ARIS & PHILLIPS HISPANIC CLASSICS

CRISTIAN ALIAGA

Music for Unknown Journeys

New and Selected Prose Poems:
Travels in Europe, Africa and the Americas

Edited and translated by

Ben Bollig

T0366436

LIVERPOOL UNIVERSITY PRESS

First published 2021 by
Liverpool University Press
4 Cambridge Street
Liverpool
L69 7ZU

This paperback edition published 2023

www.liverpooluniversitypress.co.uk

British Library Cataloguing-in-Publication data
A British Library CIP record is available

ISBN -978-1-80034-809-7 cased
ISBN -978-1-80034-810-3 paperback

Typeset by Tara Evans

Printed and bound by CPI Group (UK) Ltd, Croydon, CR0 4YY

Cover image © Ben Bollig

CONTENTS

PART TWO

The Foreign Passion (Revised and Expanded)
European and African Travels

Contents

ACKNOWLEDGMENTS

In memory of Francisco Madariaga, Manuel Quilchamal
and Guillermo Enrique Hudson.
To Sara, Paulina, Emilio and Federico.
To Ben Bollig.
To Domingo Casadei (Buenos Aires)
and Chema Morales Cerdán (Madrid).
For Andrés Cursaro, Ariel Williams
and Carlos Gamerro in Argentina.
For Eduardo Milán and Julio Recinos in Mexico;
Chris Perriam in the UK, Fernanda Peñaloza in Australia
and Concha García, Javier Gil Martín and Antonio Méndez Rubio
in Spain.
With my thanks to the Leverhume Trust and the University of Leeds.

Cristian Aliaga

***

Cristian Aliaga and Ben Bollig are grateful to The Leverhulme Trust
for supporting Cristian's visiting professorship at the University of
Leeds in 2011. We are grateful for the support and help of Paul Garner,
David Frier, Manuel Barcia Paz and Stuart Green.

St John's College, Oxford, also hosted an exhibition of 'poetry-
art' based on Aliaga's poems in 2011, and we are grateful for their
generous hospitality.

***

Too many people have helped with my work on Cristian Aliaga over the last decade for them to be named here, but my special thanks go to Fernando Sdrigotti, Rory O'Bryen, and Carlos Fonseca Grigsby for their comments and suggestions – though any errors that remain are mine and mine alone.

Chris Perriam and Fernanda Peñaloza also played instrumental roles in different ways. Thanks are also due to Carlos Fonseca Suárez and Catherine Boyle for their support. Alejandro Crotto, Nancy Fernández, and Edgardo Berg offered indispensable help when I visited Argentina in September 2014, a trip that would not have been possible without the help of The Society of Author's K. Blundell Award, for which I am most grateful. The University of Oxford and my two colleges, St Catherine's and St John's, offered me sabbatical terms in 2013 and 2020. I am grateful to the Leverhulme Trust for granting me a Research Fellowship in 2015–16 and to Rich Rabone, Alex Beard, Rachel Robinson and Carlos Fonseca Grigsby for replacing me in teaching duties at various stages. Thanks also go to Kit Caless and Gary Budden at Influx for backing the first Aliaga prose-poetry collection, *The Foreign Passion*.

Above all, I would like to thank Cristian Aliaga himself, for his unstinting help and support over the years.

Ben Bollig
Oxford, 2020

INTRODUCTION

Cristian Aliaga (b. 1962, Tres Cuervos, Province of Buenos Aires) is a writer, journalist, publisher, and lecturer. Unlike most important contemporary Argentine writers, Aliaga is based not in Buenos Aires, but in Chubut Province, in the far south. As well as a highly respected poet, Aliaga is also a master of a genre that we might call the travel prose-poem. Linked to the traditions of travel writing, politically-committed poetry, and the sociological essay – all with deep roots in Argentina – Aliaga's mini-chronicles, difficult fully to classify, give an intensely emotional, yet precise vision of specific sites in Argentina, the Americas, North Africa and Europe.

Aliaga's early work, four collections of free-verse poetry, went to press with Último reino, an influential publisher of the post-dictatorship period. They formed part of a neo-romantic revival in poetry in Argentina during the 1980s and early 1990s. 2002 was a turning point for Aliaga as a writer: he published a well-received anthology of his early work alongside the collection of prose poems, *Música desconocida para viajes* (*Unknown Music for Journeys*), which would become his best known book and be republished multiple times. This collection, here for the first time represented in a substantial translation into English, marked a breakthrough for the poet, as he combined a highly personal, emotive gaze, with documentary realist depictions of the sites that he visited – in the south, and across the Americas.

In his essays and poetry, Aliaga explores the region best known to English speakers as Patagonia. His prose writing, and his multiple projects in journalism and publishing, investigate the possibilities of creation and communication outside the metropolis. As one of the founders of the newspaper *El extremo sur de la Patagonia* and its cultural supplement, *Confines*, Aliaga traces links between forgotten or damaged places: the Western Sahara, Palestine, and Patagonia itself. His writing invites us to consider the possibilities of cultural activism in a space that is at once exploited and ignored by international interests. His poetry, meanwhile, interrogates both contemporary neoliberal capitalist development in the south, and its historical precursors, such as the nineteenth-century 'Campaign of the Desert' to claim indigenous lands for the Argentine state. It attempts to resist their effects, in particular the erasure of cultures, writings, histories, and ways of life.

Aliaga's writing draws on a long tradition of political poetry in Latin America. One might argue that poetry in the region – from early epics like Alonso de Ercilla's sixteenth-century *Araucaniad*, through the romantic verse of Esteban Echeverría, to Pablo Neruda's *Canto general* – has always been political. But starting in the 1960s and 70s, with writers like Ernesto Cardenal, Roque Dalton, and Argentina's Juan Gelman, there emerges a distinctive tendency for poets to both engage actively in political struggles and to shift their writing towards a wider audience and to urgent contemporary themes. These writers, and the aesthetic movements they promoted – in particularly Ernesto Cardenal's *exteriorismo*, a style of writing that eschewed adornment and metaphor for plain style and direct engagement with the world around the poet – are still influential.

Perhaps as a result of enforced censorship and self-censorship, and the widespread destruction to the cultural sphere during the last military dictatorship, the 1980s saw a reaction against 'social', 'committed' or 'militant' poetry. This came in the form of a highly mannered, allusive, even hermetic mode of 'neo-baroque' (or *neobarroco*) writing, associated with writers such as Arturo Carrera and Néstor Perlongher. But these years also witnessed, surprisingly, what Perlongher himself called a 'secret poetry boom': the emergence of new writers, presses, magazines, and other spaces for poetry. In his twenties, Aliaga was very much part of this emergent scene, though he has never belonged to a particular movement or group, fashioning himself as something of a lone wolf. His eccentric position – as a newspaper editor and lecturer, over 1,000 miles from Buenos Aires – is no doubt a factor.

The 1980s and 90s in Argentine poetry witnessed polemics between proponents of the *neobarroco* style and an alternative objectivist (*objetivista*) mode. *Neobarroco* poetry focused on the materiality and sensuousness of language, with reference points ranging from the Spanish Golden Age poet Luis de Góngora, through to twentieth-century writers such as Federico García Lorca, the Cuban José Lezama Lima, and Brazil's *neo-concretistas* or neo-concrete poets. *Objetivismo*, in contrast, concentrated on the creation of objects in language. Its writers and theorists – Daniel García Helder and Osvaldo Aguirre in particular – reacted to the excess and sensuality of the *neobarroco* with poetry stripped of all supposedly unnecessary components, including metaphors and even, at times, adjectives or adverbs. Literary references were mostly to Anglophone poets, not least Ezra Pound (whom Cardenal had translated in the early 1980s for a widely read 1983 Spanish-language anthology published by Madrid's Visor), William Carlos Williams, and Louis Zukofsky. *Objetivismo* played a central role in the emergence of a vibrant poetry scene in the late 1980s and 1990s, around the poetry newspaper *Diario de poesía*.

The last fifteen or twenty years have witnessed an upsurge in poetry writing and publishing in Argentina, in spite – or even because – of the economic and political hardships of the 1990s and early 2000s – and again today. Recent Argentine poetry demonstrates a striking and novel return of the political. A writer like Sergio Raimondi, in his *Poesía civil* (2001) uses carefully measured, classically inspired, blank verse to examine the effects of global capitalism on his home town of Bahía Blanca on the Atlantic coast. Andi Nachon draws the drifting lines of urban wandering to assess both spatial changes in the city and the possibilities for mass protest and political activism. Martín Gambarotta, in a series of collections, uses precise, stripped down verse, including poetic equations, to analyse the political scene since the 1990s. Other poets link their work explicitly to cultural and political activism, be it the cardboard recycling publisher Eloísa Cartonera, and the racially and sexually provocative poetry of its co-founder Washington Cucurto, or the prison poetry workshops of the group Yonofui ('It wasn't me') run by the poet María Medrano. Perhaps most importantly, as Aliaga's work often demonstrates, there is a singular and integral connection between themes, form, and circulation in much of the best recent Argentine poetry. His writing combines the *neobarroco* interest in the intricacies of language and its emotional effects; the neoromantic sense of scale and drama; and objectivist precision. Like his near contemporary Sergio Raimondi, Aliaga foregrounds a strong documentary element in his poetry.

As well as his poetry and criticism, Aliaga has published a number of essays on the politics and culture of Patagonia. Here he taps into another tradition in Argentina, and Latin America more widely: the political or sociological essay. For many specialists, the founding text of Latin American literature is by Domingo Sarmiento, a teacher and journalist who would go on to become president: *Facundo, or, Civilization and Barbarism in the Argentine Pampas*. His great rival in ideas among political liberals in Argentina in the mid-1800s was another essayist, Juan Bautista Alberdi. And the essay form – long, often painstakingly researched prose studies of contemporary problems and the potential solutions, would be continued into the twentieth century by the likes of Ezequiel Martínez Estrada, Arturo Jauretche and Beatriz Sarlo. To the essayistic tradition in Argentina, Aliaga has added a performative element, creating a multi-media staged reflection on twenty-first century 'land wars' in Argentina, premiered at the Teatro Cervantes, Argentina's National Theatre, in Buenos Aires, in September 2017, and then touring the provinces.[1]

There is a further inescapable presence in Aliaga's prose poems: travel writing. Charles Darwin is perhaps the most famous English traveller to have visited and written on the far south in the nineteenth century, but he was just one of dozens whose texts were published in European capitals and, in many cases, then translated back into Spanish for local audiences. In the twentieth-century, Bruce Chatwin's *In Patagonia* became the obligatory reference for those, local or international, who wanted to find out about life in the distant

---

1   See Aliaga's work on the 'Land Wars' in Patagonia https://medium.com/@j_lacs/las-guerras-por-la-tierra-en-la-patagonia-del-siglo-xxi-a8f13943c33c; a version in English is available in *Journal of Latin American Cultural Studies*, translated by Philip Derbyshire.

south. Aliaga, in contrast, draws on the political investigations of his fellow countryman Osvaldo Bayer, whose four-volume study of *La Patagonia rebelde* – the strikes and subsequent violent military repression of rural workers in the early 1920s – tells the politically conflicted history of the south.

Aliaga makes no secret of his literary and artistic references, noting them in epigraphs before collections and individual poems. These include the paintings of Francis Bacon, viewed on a visit to Dublin; or sculptures by Jaume Plensa seen at the Yorkshire Sculpture Park. Three writers are particularly worth mentioning. The first is Matsuo Bashō, the Japanese master of *haiku*, whose collection of travel sketches, *The Narrow Road to the Deep North*, combined observations in prose with verse by the author and those he met or who accompanied him along the way. In these, as his translator Nobuyuki Yuasa observes, "prose and *haiku* illuminate like two mirrors held up facing each other." The second is W. G. Sebald, and while it is his *Natural History of Destruction* that is referenced here, perhaps his literal, historical, and imaginative tour of the past and present of a vastly expanded East Anglia, *The Rings of Saturn*, functions as a more obvious precursor for Aliaga's own travel sketches. The third is John Berger, whose ability to combine prose poetry with a photographic sense of place can be felt acutely in *And Our Faces, My Heart, Brief as Photos*; mentioned in one poem, he is a haunting presence throughout Aliaga's work.[2] Contemporary British writers are not absent, either: the writer and artist Laura Oldfield and her stunning 'zine-cum-state of the nation address, *Savage Messiah*; and Mark Fisher, aka k-punk, the philosopher, music critic, and author of *Capitalist Realism*, who died tragically young in 2017. A further echo can be found in the recent work of Tom Pickard, and his collection 2018 *Fiends Fell*, a contemporary British response to Bashō's poetry-prose mix, situated in rural Cumbria. And there are other names too, from literature and music – Harold Pinter, The Smiths, Leyland Kirby (aka The Caretaker), and The Clash.

One name missing from this constellation but ineluctable in

---

2   I am grateful to Rory O'Bryen for pointing out this reference to me.

Aliaga's personal canon, is Juan Carlos Bustriazo Ortiz (1929–2010). Bustriazo, perhaps the epitome of a marginal poet, spent much of his life wandering Buenos Aires province and the Pampas. He spent the years after his military service drifting from friend's house to friend's house, writing prodigiously, publishing little or nothing, and drinking heavily. But he carried with him a portfolio containing his entire life's works, which at one stage came to comprise sixty unpublished books of poetry, and which he managed to lose, supposedly left at a female friend's house. Aliaga and colleagues worked to compile Bustriazo's works, rescuing lost texts, and publishing new editions of published and unpublished works. In the early 2000s Bustriazo emerged as something of an iconic figure in Patagonian literature, in particular because of his life of poetic wandering. His life, like that of the many migrants in Aliaga's work, reflects both modern economic reality and the long history of vagrancy in Argentina.

The geographical context of Aliaga's work is important as, alongside the historical literary and anthropological conquest of the south, a new conquest has been taking place in recent years. As he said in his talk, 'The Land Wars in Patagonia':

> The 'war' for the land is fierce and on-going. On one side there are the descendants of the Mapuche and Tehuelche peoples – and there are only a few speakers of the indigenous languages left – and those other Argentines who are denied even the smallest piece of land. On the other are those who have owned the land since the so-called Conquest of the Desert [in the 1870s], who came to appropriate vast areas, refusing to recognise their former occupants and in many cases their own laws. Ever since there has been an immense tension between legality and legitimacy.
>
> At present, indigenous communities are resisting evictions from their ancestral lands in a total of twelve Argentine provinces, involving 9 million hectares. First Peoples – Tehuelches, Mapuches, Selknam, Yamanas, and other – who were once in control of their territories are now being evicted from them. Today, their descendants are fighting for their identity and property, as they are subjected to actions by the State that massively disadvantage them politically.
>
> The vanguard of concentrated capitalism is built on a continuous

process of territorial purchase and extraction of natural resources that threatens national sovereignty much more profoundly than any claim by the Mapuche people. The legal, institutional and political framework turns out to be inadequate to deal with new scenarios and different cultures. Out of negligence, prejudice or ideological stance. Social protest is being 'criminalized' and judges and legal agents are being co-opted by global business which has a tremendously seductive material power. The Law acts in a manifestly unequal way when it comes to land recovery and the demands of the descendants of the Mapuche and Tehuelche, migrants without resources, and the inhabitants of marginal neighbourhoods in the cities. All these sectors find access to the land impossible as it becomes more and more expensive through foreign investment. Meanwhile, the towns and provincial governments turn the demands for housing and land into a bureaucratic nightmare.

'Deep' ecology is also emerging as a strategy of 'ethical' appropriation. Several foundations and NGOs have been denounced as complicit with the business interests that finance them. In a sort of perverse symmetry, business people who have a vision of 'conservation' are acquiring enormous, untouchable territories in order to 'take care of them'. These are resources that ought to form part of the inheritance of humanity as a whole. In practice, they are being taken 'away' from Argentines and Chileans who are presumed to be incapable of looking after and conserving them and to lack the necessary resources to do so, [to be taken 'care of' by big business]. Douglas Tompkins, a citizen of the US, has created a sort of bi-national 'province' of thousands of hectares in Santa Cruz (Argentina) and Palena (Chile).

As Eva-Lynn Jagoe writes in *The End of the World As They Knew It. Writing Experiences of the Argentine South* (2008):

Large tracts of the South have been sold to foreign investors. One of the most notorious of these sales was made to the Italian clothing company Benetton, the largest landholder in Argentina. The nine hundred thousand hectares of land bought by the company have traditionally been inhabited by Mapuche-Tehuelches, who continue to live in Patagonia despite the rhetoric of extermination that prevails in Argentine history. These indigenous people are in the process of disputing Benetton's land claims. Other large tracts of Patagonia are owned by CNN magnate Ted Turner, philanthropist George Soros, North American eco-investors, multinational companies, and movie stars.

What is more, the purchase of these lands has often been facilitated by, firstly, what amount in most cases to dubious land claims by vendors who frequently have no link to the land in question and, secondly, a collapse in exchange rates that resulted from an economic crisis in large part caused by the adoption of economic policies sponsored by the IMF and the World Bank, and which were singularly unfavourable for the average Argentine. Ownership of the land implies rights that exclude indigenous and native peoples, and may even include the most valuable of all resources: subterranean deposits and water. These struggles have only intensified in recent years, with the government of Mauricio Macri eager to cosy up to foreign investors and an increasing tendency towards violent suppression of dissent, as seen in the tragic cases of activists like Santiago Maldonado and the continued persecution of the indigenous leader Facundo Jones Huala.

In 2011, Cristian Aliaga took up an eight-month visiting professorship at the University of Leeds. As a poet long interested in travel writing, and who in *Música desconocida* had pioneered a form of prose poetry that could capture politically significant and emotionally affecting moments from his journeys, his stay in Europe offered the chance to turn the centre's gaze back on itself. As he had done in Patagonia, Aliaga travelled to those places that exist and do not exist: former mining communities, destroyed in the 1980s; identikit towns with their franchise high streets; run-down suburban railway stations; and the open spaces of the Yorkshire moors. He visited sites of conflict, such as the Falls Road in Belfast; places of poetic significance, such as Dylan Thomas's house, or Federico García Lorca's likely grave; and the centres of European culture that those from the periphery – and in his case the periphery of the periphery – are told to admire.

The poems that emerged from his European residency are marked by an evolution in his poetic form. The prose poem still dominates, but it is more marked by sharp changes of rhythm; cut, concentrated phrases; and a certain harshness, even brutality, of language and gaze. These are poems coloured by existential uprooting, uncertainty, and the sense of being lost. If *Unknown Music* examined the effects of neoliberalism in the Americas, the results of shocks, crises, and austerity over the decades of the 1980s and 1990s, *The Foreign Passion* moves from the guinea pig to the main trial, from the effects of capitalism red in tooth and claw on the edge of the edge, to its results in the central countries where it is theorised and to which the profits made elsewhere return for the good of the few.

Aliaga asks questions about travel itself: what is travel? Why travel? What do we seek? In his visits to museums and galleries, he adds to their order and organization a touch of the improvised, the haphazard, and the perilous. What is the purpose of travel when every day, across the globe, thousands of people are uprooted, made homeless, or lose their country, or when millions already – in Syria, the Western Sahara, or Palestine – have no home or country to speak of? How to hear and write these stories without imposing our own? Each poem, with Aliaga's unique, disquieting voice, gives a home for the unheard stories of today's dispossessed, with all their beauty and pain.

***

Aliaga's form and vocabulary present few problems for the translator, other than to recreate the repetitions (especially of title and phrase) that characterise many poems. But his phrasing is more difficult to render. Readers of his works who know Spanish may often be struck by the 'almost heard' feeling of his language. Aliaga takes clichés and set phrases, or vernacular snippets, and alters them slightly, leaving the original phrase visible, but changed or even damaged. The problem for the translator is to leave evidence of this particular work on words, without creating a jarring effect beyond the discomfiture caused by and in the original. I have opted throughout to downplay this effect, with a view to comprehension, but not to the extent of over-naturalising or over-domesticating Aliaga's poems in their English versions.

Another Aliaga hallmark is syntactic: the prose-poem lends itself to compression, and he often suppresses connectives or conjunctions. Sometimes such omissions create a form of anacoluthon, where a sentence starts with one implicit grammatical structure and ends with another. In Aliaga's case, it is because the link has been left out between clauses that in vernacular prose would be further apart. There is, it hardly needs to be said, no padding in an Aliaga prose-poem. The result in Spanish can be disconcerting, as a poem turns sharply on a phrase, or the reader is forced to build a mental bridge. I have tried, as much as possible, to respect these effects, only intervening when the most 'literal' version left implicit or even wholly unsaid something that was relatively apparent to the reader of the Spanish. The aim throughout has been to make the poet comprehensible to the reader of English, without losing too many of the original's peculiarities that are so vital to its emotional impact.

To illustrate my approach, it is worth offering some examples, in some cases drawn from the exchanges with the readers of earlier drafts of these translations. Having spent so long translating Aliaga, more or less in isolation, these second and third opinions were vital. In the poem *Los caminos equivocados*, the phrase "A cada rato preguntamos ¿vamos bien, vamos bien?" had originally been rendered as "Every so often we ask, are we going ok, are we going ok?" One reader, a bilingual Spanish and English speaker, who has lived mostly in Central and North American, suggested a change: something along the lines of, "We constantly ask, are we going ok, are we going ok?" This seemed to capture better the process of doubting and questioning described in the poem but it needed further nuance in English. Another reader (a native English speaker, but with excellent Spanish) proposed "are we on the right track" or "going in the right direction". After some consideration, the final version reads, "We constantly ask, are we on the right track, are we on the right track?" with the a-k sound partially reflecting the internal -amos rhyme of the original.

In *El sol enfría*, the issue at hand was more literary. Here I struggled with the very first word, "El páramo" – a term that will be familiar to readers of Latin American literature from Juan Rulfo's novel *Pedro Páramo*. In earlier drafts it was a 'wasteland', but as one reader pointed out this conjured up echoes of T. S. Eliot that are not necessarily present in the original poem: "I just wonder whether it doesn't create a link with Eliot here (*La tierra baldía*) which might not (or might it?) be in the original. Is 'moorland' just wrong? Or plain?" I spent some time looking at images of the setting of the poem, Cotagaita, Bolivia, before settling on 'bleak plateau' and then 'plateau' as a more neutral, but still visually significant, term.

There were problems, too, of cultural reference. One simple problem was the word 'siesta', as in the poem *La siesta de los vivos* (*vivos* is living; in Argentina it also carries a sense of cunning). The *siesta* is a culturally specific practice – which the English word 'nap' does not quite capture, as well as sounding like a term from a different type of text. The title had been translated throughout as '*The Sleep of the Living*'; the logic behind this was that the poem in question is explicitly set in Spain, during the day, and thus any sleep mentioned in it is by necessity a siesta. Of my readers, only one picked me up on this: "Siesta would work as well, if you want to be more specific". I experimented with a change to original version, but felt that this did not work: it sounded *untranslated*, or like *translationese* – and in the end, the line runs thus: "Then, they leave, smiling towards the sun, the cool air, the stew that will taste better on their return, thinking about the summer wine and the sleep of the living." British readers may note a translation *gain*, as for those of a certain vintage, "summer wine" is unmistakably comic – not out of keeping with the mood of the original poem, which mixes fatalism and dry humour.

Some of the problems faced by the translator are very specific. The poem *Armas largas inocentes* describes a trip to the Royal Armouries Museum in Leeds. Initially the title phrase had been translated as '*Innocent Firearms*'. One reader observed: "Not shotguns? Or rifles? I mean in order to capture the 'armas largas' connotation..." And after some consideration I realized that 'firearms' is too general, too vague, and that readers needed to be able to visualize a specific gun. I lived in Leeds for a number of years and had visited the museum in question, so could picture exactly what Aliaga was referencing. The final version is '*Innocent Rifles*'; rifles are included in that particular display in the museum. Again, there is a gain: an echo of The Jam's song, *The Eton Rifles*.

As mentioned earlier, Aliaga takes his titles from the text of the poem and this can throw up some of the knottiest problems for a translator. One poem, set in Belfast, is entitled *El dolor que acuna*. On first reading, that means, '*The Pain that Cradles*'. In the poem, however, the phrase says something different: "Quién podría desprenderse de todo el dolor que acuna, sin sentir que el mundo desaparecerá por eso, para siempre, con la belleza adherida." – "Who could let go of all the pain they cradle, without feeling that the world will disappear with it, forever, with all the beauty too." As one reader pointed out, "In the original title it's the pain that cradles, not them cradling the pain. Still not sure how I'd resolve this but I wanted you to be aware." I checked this with Aliaga: my version is grammatically correct but the problem of the title remains unresolved. After much consideration, I concluded that I needed to stick to the poem's text, and the title had to follow from that. So instead it reads '*The Pain They Cradle*'. Sadly, the ambiguity of the original is lost.

Finally, one encounters problems that can never be fully resolved. In the poem, *Los lugares fugaces*, we read: "No hay como la belleza imposible de describir." My first translation was, "There's nothing like beauty that's impossible to describe." However, with no violence to Spanish grammar, this could also be rendered as: "There's nothing like the impossible beauty of description." One of my readers pointed this out; he added, "However, I think it could be either (or both!), to be honest." So I tried, "There's nothing like the beauty of impossible description." Part of the logic was that there exists a slight ambiguity in the English, too – the impossible description could be beautiful, or the beauty could be impossible to describe. To this second version, another reader responded: "Wouldn't 'the impossible beauty of description' be more faithful here?" In the end, I reverted to "There's nothing like the impossible beauty of description." Sometimes these knots cannot be wholly unpicked. As Borges put it, in a discussion of translations of Homer, the concept of a *definitive text* belongs only to religion or tiredness.

***

A note on the sources: *Música desconocida* was first published in 2002 by Deldragón of Buenos Aires with a prologue by Francisco Madariaga. An expanded version was published by Desde la gente (Buenos Aires) in 2009. A few of the poems were included in Spanish original and English translation in the selection *La causa clínica/ The Clinical Cause* (Manchester University, 2011). A number of the poems included here in part 2 were first published (in earlier versions) in *The Foreign Passion/La pasión extranjera* (London: Influx, 2016). A complete Spanish-language version of *La pasión extranjera* was published by Espacio Hudson (Rada Tilly, Chubut) in 2018. I have also written about Aliaga's work in *Modern Argentine Poetry. Displacement, Exile, Migration* (University of Wales Press, 2011).

PART ONE

Unknown Music for Journeys
North and South American Travels

*Those who steer a boat across the sea or drive a horse over the
earth till they succumb to the weight of the years, spend every
minute of their lives travelling.*

Matsuo Bashō
(trans. Nobuyuki Yuasa)

*With us, the
tossed about, yet
traveling:
the one
unharmed,
not usurpable,
rebellious
grief.*

Paul Celan
(trans. Pierre Joris)

Surely I'm going to find a path.

Yves Bonnefoy
(trans. Emily Grosholz)

Every ruin looks something like a temple.

Hugo Mujica

EL PRÍNCIPE DE DOWN

¿Genever?, ¿scotch? inquiere en su bar destartalado el bolichero de Deseado. El canoso sentado a la barra del bar podría tomar hasta lo indeseable, por eso no responde. Beba, concede como en un responso el bolichero al empujar un vaso de boca ancha servido con ginebra destilada lejos de Holanda, lejos de Puerto Deseado. Beba, ordena, y el otro no resiste porque no podría. Al pasar las cortinas, el olor rancio se extiende, es orín y humano estiércol, se pega a la ropa del príncipe de Down que rasca la ventana. En calzones, la pierna derecha se le mueve sin control. La canción de la radio será siempre lejana para él, como las palabras que su padre lanza como adormideras para desear su muerte, la suya, que no llegará a entender, ni cuando suceda. La ventana será por siempre el mundo que sus dedos no han de tocar.

(Puerto Deseado)

THE DOWN PRINCE

Jenever? Scotch? asks the barman in his rundown joint in Deseado. The grey-haired man propping up the bar could drink beyond what's desirable, so he doesn't answer. Drink, concedes the barman like a prayer for the dead, as he pushes over a wide-rimmed glass filled with gin, distilled far from Holland, far from Puerto Deseado. Drink, he orders, and the man doesn't resist, because he couldn't. As the curtains are drawn, the rancid smell wafts out: urine and human dung, which sticks to the clothes of the Down Prince who scratches the window. In his underwear, his right leg moves uncontrollably. The song on the radio will always be distant for him, like the words his father casts like opium poppies wishing his death, his, that he'll never manage to understand, even when it arrives. The window will always be the world that his fingers mustn't touch.

(Puerto Deseado, Santa Cruz, Arg.)

TRENES DESAPARECIDOS

Una luz mortecina encendida a las seis de la mañana en la soledad de la pampa seca. El sol no ha salido y la temperatura está bajo el cero del termómetro, pero el dueño tiene su gorra encasquetada y se ha puesto los mocasines, cosidos trabajosamente con hilo de atar. Su orgullo está en el mostrador y el espejo europeo, de cuatro metros cuadrados y sesenta años de antigüedad, que sirve de fondo al despacho de ginebra y Hesperidina, al extremo de una calle única de cuatro casas deshabitadas. Escancia caña quemada en copas diminutas como la luz que parece abrirse paso entre la locura de aquellos que son capaces de creer sin indicio alguno, exégetas de la repetición. Aferrado a una botella de anís se sienta en el andén a ver pasar los trenes desaparecidos. Y si alguna vez decidiera partir, ¿a quién va a dejarle el bar casi destruido, con el espejo que su padre trajo en barco, sin que se rompiera, hasta este lugar perdido en el mundo?

(Tellier)

DISAPPEARED TRAINS

A deathly light turned on at six in the morning in the loneliness of the Western Pampas. The sun isn't up and the temperature is still showing below zero, but the boss has his cap pulled down and his moccasins on, painstakingly sewn up with string. His pride rests on the counter and the European mirror, fours metres squared and 70 years old, which acts as the back of a dispensary for gin and Hesperidina,[1] at the end of the only street, with its four empty houses. He pours rum in glasses as minute as the light that seems to cut a path amid the madness of those willing to believe with no evidence, exegetes of repetition. Clinging on to a bottle of anise he sits on the platform to watch the disappeared trains go by. And if he ever decided to go, who'd he leave the bar to – almost in ruins, with the mirror his father brought on the boat, without it breaking, to this lost corner of the world.

(Tellier, Santa Cruz)

SUS ALARDES

La gente muere en todas partes, pero en los caminos no hay vida que alcance. Los huesos asomándose en las fosas de los peones asesinados, todos muertos a los veinte y a los treinta años, asoladas sus cruces por el mismo salitre que tapó sus pulmones en la vida. Las construcciones de ladrillo al borde de la ruta, los corralitos de metal pintados de blanco con las flores de plástico, el espectáculo de la muerte viajera, alardeando ella sin geografía que la desampare.

(Fitz Roy)

A SHOW

People die everywhere, but on the road there's no life that's enough. Bones sticking out from the graves of the murdered peons, all dead at twenty or thirty, their crosses dried out by the same saltpetre that smothered their lungs in life. The brick structures by the side of the road, the little metal fences painted white with their plastic flowers, the spectacle of a travelling Death, making a show with no geography to leave her undone.

(Fitz Roy, Santa Cruz)

LOS CAMINOS EQUIVOCADOS

A cada rato preguntamos: ¿vamos bien, vamos bien? Los carteles de estas rutas conducen a cualquier parte, no fueron hechos para indicar destinos ni para confiar en ellos. Dependemos del instinto, que sirve para amar pero no depara aciertos. Vamos, sin embargo, preguntando dónde, con las manos en el corazón, que sólo a veces intuye los caminos equivocados. Podemos preguntar si vamos bien, no deja de surgir una tentación, pero nadie tiene caminos para regresar gracias a las preguntas.

(Sibayo)

THE WRONG ROUTES

We constantly ask, are we on the right track, are we on the right track? The signs on these routes lead anywhere, they weren't designed to indicate destinations or to be trusted. We depend on instinct, which works for love but offers no right answers. But we go along asking where, hands on our heart, that only now and then intuits the wrong paths. We can ask how we're going, the temptation is always there, but questions have never given anyone a way back.

(Sibayo, Peru)

EL SOL ENFRÍA

El páramo no es una estela de soledad para quienes ven imágenes bajo la arena; la cara de los astros muerde el rostro de los que aspiran a soñar. El sol enfría, enfría, hasta sorprender el dolor de los imbéciles, dulces como la cara de Dios. El rostro de la soledad es ese rastro en el páramo. No ves, sólo tus párpados se atreven a lo imposible. Nadie huye como vino, con una mano en la espalda y otra cubriendo el corazón. Nadie nos ha traído hasta aquí, no podemos explicar cómo llegamos, si el vivir está siempre más allá.

(Cotagaita)

THE SUN COOLS

The bleak plateau is no trail of loneliness for those who see images beneath the sand; the mouth of the stars bites the face of those who aspire to dream. The sun cools, cools, until it surprises the imbeciles' pain, sweet as the image of God. The face of solitude is that trace on the plateau. You don't see, only your eyelids dare for the impossible. No one flees like they arrived, with one hand on their back and another covering their heart. No one brought us here, we can't explain how we arrived, if living is always further on.

(Cotagaita, Bolivia)

EL TUMBADO

Gallinas blancas picotean los cimientos del edificio inglés y sus crestas rojas son el único color que rompe la monotonía de esta nieve. Es oscuro, como una manta de barniz bajo la luz de la tarde. Ha cantado el amanecer, no puede mover un pie detrás del otro después de tanta carretera. El viento se matiza con remolinos sobre el piso de tierra. Bebe ginebra con la bombilla del mate, descansa de una turba que lo sigue en el carromato del invierno. Busca recordar su nombre, pero no hay necesidad porque lo llaman El Tumbado. Él asegura que ese adjetivo es falso. Baja su pulgar pero nadie muere.

(Estación Holdich)

FACE DOWN

White hens peck at the English building's foundations and their red combs are the only colour that breaks the monotony of this snow. It's dark, like a coat of varnish under the afternoon light. The dawn has sung, he can't move one foot after the other after so long on the road. The wind takes shape with whirlwinds on the earth floor. He drinks gin through a *mate* straw,[2] resting from a crowd following him in the winter wagon. He hunts for a memory of his name, but there's no need as they call him Face Down. He insists that the description is false. He gives a thumbs-down, but nobody dies.

(Holdich Station, Chubut)

ALGUNA VEZ VOLÓ

Pudo ser otro pájaro, pero es un cisne con el cuello negro y quebrado. Este cuerpo caliente y blanco hace dudar sobre su muerte a quien lo levanta; es la imagen de un mito y en cuatro días será una masa informe entre las piedras de la playa. Este pájaro no asume conciencia de símbolo ni de melancolía: ¿o acaso la muerte es más muerte en este cuello quebrado? Aquí, como en casi todo el planeta, el cisne es sólo un bulto que alguna vez voló y ahora se ha aquietado.

(Camarones)

ONCE IT FLEW

It might have been some other bird, but it's a swan with its neck black and snapped. This warm white body makes whoever picks it up doubt its death; it's the image of a myth and in four days will be a shapeless mass among the rocks on the beach. This bird has no awareness of symbols or of melancholy: or is death more deadly in this snapped neck? Here, as almost anywhere else on the planet, the swan is just a lump that once flew and now falls silent.

(Camarones, Chubut)

LUZ DE INVIERNO

La única luz encendida es la del invierno. El pueblo tiene una calle para recorrer, evitando que el horizonte acabe antes que uno. Dos catamaranes y los botes parecen abandonados en la arena. Un arco de caños de aluminio ha sido clavado en las rocas, al borde mismo del acantilado. ¿Quién podría atajar lo que viene de la tierra, de espaldas al mar, solo como todos los hombres a la hora de la definición, con el Atlántico a medio metro de la espalda? El viento parece estar compuesto de una sola ráfaga, una que espolvorea lo que somos, una que sacude las cien almas del pueblo tras la bajamar. Una virgen de terracota descansa dentro del hueco cavado en el cerro, con los restos de la fe.

(Puerto Pirámides)

WINTER LIGHT

The only light that's on is winter's. The town has one street to walk along, so the horizon doesn't end before you do. Two catamarans and the boats look abandoned on the sand. An arch of aluminium tubes has been rammed into the rocks, on the very edge of the cliff. Who could block what comes from the land, back turned to the sea, alone like all humans at the defining moment, with the Atlantic two feet from your back? The wind seems to consist of one single gust, one that scatters what we are, that shakes the hundred-odd souls in the town after the low-tide. A terracotta virgin rests inside a hollow carved in the hills, with what remains of faith.

(Puerto Pirámides, Chubut)

LOS LUGARES FUGACES

No hay como la belleza imposible de describir. No es decir estuve, vi, sé lo que había. Memorar el olor de las plantas que subía desde el patio interior del hotel Vucina, la escalera de madera, los pasillos que llevan a los cuartos bajo la noche oscura, el mar junto al inmenso desierto; todo eso no sirve más que para evocar lo visible. A veces sabemos que seríamos casi felices si pudiéramos quedarnos para siempre en los lugares fugaces: tal vez en esa condición la certeza se apoya, imposible de comprobar. Algo hay en la luz del desierto que azula, el horizonte se vuelve una razón de vida, el sol trae un peso tangible que parece acompasarnos en el aire.

(Tocopilla)

FLEETING PLACES

There's nothing like the impossible beauty of description. It's not saying, I came, I saw, I know what was there. To summon up the fragrance of the plants wafting up from the courtyard in the Vucina hotel, the wooden stairs, the corridors leading to rooms under the dark night, the sea alongside the immense desert; all that only serves to evoke the visible. Sometimes we know that we'd be almost happy just to stay for ever in fleeting places: perhaps that's what the certainty is based on, impossible to prove. There's a blue wash in the desert light, the horizon becomes a reason for living, the sun carries a weight you can touch that seems to match our steps in the air.

(Tocopilla, Chile)

MALEDICENCIA

El terror, el amor, porque el día pasa. Ha de pasar, aquí, con más penas de las que preveía el hombre cuyo apodo se repite en monedas y edificios. Asesinado, toman su nombre como banderola, los usos son ilimitados, las monedas llevan su permanencia. Sabía él quién era, pero no lo que podrían hacer de él ya muerto. Los visitantes quieren llevarse alguna muestra de su paso por estas tierras: eso alienta a la invención, el narrar de historias lejanas que nadie ha presenciado para venir a repetirlas ante los viajeros. Hay sin embargo un brillo que bordea las palabras de la mentira, un aire que despiden los relatos a despecho de los que hablan. Ese hombre, despeñado por la historia, saqueado por la mordida del tiempo, dejó señales que ni la maledicencia puede borrar del todo.

(Matanzas)

SLANDER

Terror, love, because the day goes by. It has to go by, here, with more sorrows than those he foresaw, his nickname repeated on coins and buildings.[3] Murdered, they take his name as a banner, the uses are unlimited, the coins carry his permanence. He knew who he was, but not what they could do with him once dead. Visitors want to take away evidence of his time in this land: that spurs on inventions, the telling of distant stories nobody saw to be repeated once more for the travellers. But something shines on the edge of these lying words, an air given off by the stories in spite of their tellers. That man, history's reject, ransacked by the bite of time, left signs that not even slander can fully erase.

(Matanzas, Cuba)

BORRACHO O ABRASADO

¿Hay portadores de inocencia? Bajo el inmenso sol, amasa pan sobre un árbol cortado, y canta, inconsciente del mundo o valiente a costa de la inocencia. Podrá morir alguna de estas noches, borracho o abrasado por la estupidez del orgullo, pero nadie ha de dejar en él nada parecido al dolor. La vida es justa con quienes aprenden a desconocerla.

(Niebla)

DRUNK OR SCORCHED

Are there carriers of innocence? Under the vast sun, he kneads bread on a felled tree, and sings, unaware of the world or brave at the cost of innocence. He could die any one of these nights, drunk or scorched by the stupidity of pride, but no one should impose on him anything like pain. Life is fair to those who learn to ignore it.

(Niebla, Chile)

PASIÓN HEREJE

Chatarra del imperio americano. Tierras congeladas, autopistas que conducen a ciudades idénticas. Vagones abandonados a la quietud, Oldsmobiles, Fords, objetos de la industria que el tiempo oxida hasta volverlos aptos para el recuerdo. Aún no valen nada. Casas montadas por kilómetro, galpones escorados, restos de carteles que relucen idénticos en todos los rincones de este país-planeta que desconoce toda exterioridad. Camiones incontables detenidos bajo el invierno sin gente a la vista, moteles ruteros mojados e inmóviles, acumulaciones y desmesuras en serie, en trance bélico con la estética. Originales de metal que el planeta calca con pasión hereje para repetir en la lejanía.

(Waxahachie)

HERETICAL PASSION

The American empire's junk. Frozen lands, highways that lead to identical cities. Wagons abandoned to quietude, Oldsmobiles, Fords, industry's objects that time rusts into shapes fit for memory. Still they're worthless. Houses built by the kilometre, propped-up warehouses, vestiges of billboards that look identical in all corners of this planet-country that ignores anything outside. Trucks you can't count under a winter with no one in sight, roadside motels damp and immobile, pile-ups and hype in series, at war with aesthetics. Metal originals that the whole world calques with heretical passion to repeat far away.

(Waxahachie, TX)

VUELO SOBRE LOS MAPAS

La isla, encerrada en su bruma, desafía al exterior, niega la existencia del mundo que se insinúa en la otra orilla. Cientos de flamencos en decenas de lenguas de tierra desdibujan los límites y dejan su pisada sobre los mapas, dibujos irrelevantes. Esta tierra-agua, espacio sin separación, está dotada de antiguos elementos mágicos, imposibles de nombrar sin el ansia de la fe, que los vuelve reales. Los barcos están habitados de otra presencia, el movimiento de los marineros chilotes es medido, religioso en sentido profundo, remite al misterio. Nadie cantaría en cubierta, el viento y las mareas sólo devuelven lo que beben. De las casas plantadas sobre el mar sube algo más que humo, hay una bruma que convierte a los bueyes, a los pájaros marinos, al labrador que trabaja inconmovible bajo el aguacero, en aires del espíritu, otra cosa.

(Curaco de Vélez)

FLIGHT OVER THE MAPS

The island, enclosed in its fog, defies the outside, denies the existence of the world that insinuates itself on the other bank. Hundreds of flamingos on dozens of strips of land blur the edges and leave their footprints over the maps, irrelevant drawings. The water-land, space free of divides, is blessed with ancient magical beings, impossible to name without the hunger of faith, which turns them real. The boats are inhabited by another presence, the movement of the Chiloé sailors is measured, religious in a deep sense, harking back to mystery. No one would sing on deck, the wind and the tides only give back what they drink. From the houses planted by the sea there emerges something more than smoke, there's a fog that turns the cattle, the sea birds, the labourer who works unperturbed under the downpour, into airs of the spirit, into something else.

(Curaco de Vélez, Chile)

MUSEO

Velan el fantasma de un escritor famoso que durmió en esta cama de caños de hierro. Él ha visto fugazmente estos mismos tamariscos sacudidos por el viento, la casa que interrumpe la línea del horizonte; se sentó a comer la única carne que sirven aquí, la del cordero, sobre este mantel de hule. La dueña del lugar ha sumado a su museo personal un libro y una foto del escritor inglés que durmió en su cama. Allí amarillea, lejos de la celebridad, ese libro escrito en otro idioma con la autoridad de quien cree haber visto el mundo repetido varias veces, junto a las bolas de ceniza extraídas del estómago de un caballo, huevos de avestruz, botellas de Hesperidina y ginebra Bols, lápidas de cementerios abandonados y un afiche de troperos anarquistas.

(Los Tamariscos)

MUSEUM

They mourn the ghost of a famous writer who slept in this iron-framed bed. He's seen, fleetingly, these same tamarisks shaken by the wind, the house that interrupts the line of the horizon; he sat down to eat the only meat that's served here, lamb, on this oilskin tablecloth. The woman who owns the place has added to her personal museum a book and a photo by the English writer who slept in her bed. There, far from fame, the book turns yellow, written in another language with the authority of someone who thinks he's seen the world repeated many times, alongside balls of ash removed from a horse's stomach, ostrich eggs, bottles of Hesperidina and Bols, headstones in abandoned graveyards and a poster of anarchist gauchos.[4]

(Los Tamariscos, Chubut)

GEOGRAFÍAS

Si el paisaje desaparece, queda el alma. Tal vez, el paisaje en su parte interior, o el paisaje en blanco, la que no tiene correspondencia; no hay complemento dentro del cuerpo. Queda todo y a la vez lo que persiste no es todo, pero de todas maneras eso es la ilusión. Las palabras son paisaje, porque la palabra 'desierto' da existencia, aunque apenas sea estación abandonada, como río que dibuja las lenguas. Si logramos que el paisaje desaparezca, queda el río sin palabras en el medio; quedan arbustos del desierto sin oraciones que los perturben. El paisaje a secas no es literatura. Es lo que respiramos. La parte inferior del alma es el paisaje, no es lo que se ve, sino lo que dura cuando ya pasamos, cuando no queda ni el recuerdo de lo que intuimos al pasar. Nadie ve sino espejos; pero los cerros, picadas, aguas, molinos, alerzales, vientos, montes, bajamares, lluvias, roqueríos, no son paisaje sino espejos pulidos. Ahí vemos lo que no existe, geografías de aquello que no es posible nombrar.

(Los Altares)

GEOGRAPHIES

If the landscape disappears, the soul remains. Perhaps, the landscape in its interior, or the landscape as a blank, without anything to correspond to; there is no complement inside the body. Everything remains but at the same time what persists isn't everything, but all the same that's the illusion. Words are landscape, because the word 'desert' lends existence, even though it's only an abandoned station, like a river that sketches languages. If we make the landscape disappear, there's still the wordless river in the middle; the desert bushes remain with no prayers to disturb them. The landscape on its own isn't literature. It's what we breathe. The lower region of the soul is landscape, it's not what we see, but what lasts when we've passed by, when there's no longer any memory of what we made out as we passed. We see only mirrors; but the hills, trails, waters, mills, larches, winds, mountains, low tides, rains, rocky shores, are not landscapes but polished mirrors. There we see what doesn't exist, geographies of something impossible to name.

(Los Altares, Chubut)

UN MAR QUE TIEMBLE

Al extremo de la costanera, el barco devuelto por el mar reposa para siempre, inmóvil en un ángulo de sesenta grados. El resto de los buques – varados en la arena a la espera de una marea que los ponga a flote – constituyen la graduación hacia el naufragio. El óxido es el verdadero tripulante, apenas deja pasar resabios de rojos y amarillos, patrón de tiempo. Ostreros y gaviotas de lomo engrasado picotean las chapas que aún sirven para flotar. La palabra 'puerto' es horizonte para quienes divisan desde la orilla velámenes y luces lejanas al otro lado de la mar océano, que no existen. La mirada pierde su orientación, pero no es chatarra lo que se ve sino movimiento, viajes desesperados en busca de un mar que tiemble con nosotros.

(Comodoro Rivadavia)

A SEA THAT TREMBLES

At the other end of the promenade, the boat returned by the sea sits forever, immobile at a sixty-degree angle. The rest of the boats – beached on the sand awaiting a high tide to float them – make up the different grades of shipwreck. Rust is their real crewmember, scarcely letting past an aftertaste of red and yellow, the pattern of time. Oystercatchers and greased-back gulls peck at the metals that are still able to float. The word 'port' is a horizon for those who see from the shore sails and distant lights on the other side of the Ocean Sea, that don't exist. The gaze loses its bearings, but it's not junk it sees but movement, desperate journeys searching for a sea that trembles with us.

(Comodoro Rivadavia, Chubut)

LA POSE EXACTA

Carteles que llevan a pueblos tan cercanos al costado de la ruta como para existir en la memoria, pero tan lejanos que nadie llegará a pisarlos. Esos nombres esconden imágenes desconocidas, salvadas su realidad y la modestia por unos pocos kilómetros. Unas luces titilan donde la vista no alcanza del todo: ahí están los pueblos cuyos motivos no llevan a los viajeros a desviarse. No sabe nadie el trazado de las calles, la pose exacta de los parroquianos en los boliches, la dirección del viento que mueve los árboles en este mediodía, la canción que canta esa mujer que hace pan hasta morir; el rostro del chico que saldrá del pueblo para recorrer el mundo.

(Tolhuin)

THE EXACT POSE

Signs pointing to towns close enough to the side of the road to exist in memory, but far enough that no one will ever set foot there. Those names hide unknown images, their reality and modesty covered by a few miles.[5] Some lights twinkle beyond clear sight: there are the towns whose motifs are not worth a traveller's detour.[6] No one knows the lay of the streets, the exact pose of the locals in the bars, the direction of the wind that moves the trees at noon now, the song sung by the woman there who makes bread until she dies; the face of the boy who'll leave the town to travel the world.

(Tolhuin, Tierra del Fuego)

ÚLTIMOS HEREJES

Nos están alambrando el campo los raza blanca, señor, dijo el cacique Quilchamal a Roca, el general. Antes había mucho animal, yegua, vaca, oveja, le dijo, pero ahora dejan a los animales del lado de adentro de los alambres y a mi gente afuera. Yo le digo con respeto esta cuestión, señor general, yo para qué voy a hablar mentiras. No sería hombre, entonces. ¿Un general sabe eso? El problema de recordar es el temblor, piensa el cacique mientras avanza hacia Chalía. Cuida de no dormirse, de no caer sobre el caballo que avanza pisoteando las mentiras del general, la baba de coroneles y mercachifles que ha acumulado el siglo con su viento sobre la planicie. Quilchamal duerme, en realidad, aferrado al animal que lo conduce a la muerte en un malón sin esperanza. Duerme en medio de un malón ya sin lanza ni enemigos, para la muerte basta el viento helado y la nieve que cae sobre los últimos tehuelches, puntitos en medio de la pampa, animales sin leña ni carne; últimos herejes de la llanura repleta de rocas.

(Lago Blanco, en memoria de Manuel Quilchamal)

THE LAST HERETICS

They're fencing off the land on us, the white skins, sir, said the cacique Quilchamal to Roca, the General.[7] Before, there was lots of animals, mares, cows, sheep, he told him, but now they leave the animals on the inside of the wires and my people on the outside. I say this question to you with respect, Mr General, why would I speak lies. I wouldn't be a man, then. A general knows that? The problem of remembering is the trembling, thinks the cacique as he heads towards Chalía. He takes care not to sleep, not to drop on the horse that tramples over the lies of the general, the drool of colonels and hucksters that the century's stored up with its wind over the plain. Quilchamal sleeps, in reality, arms around the animal that carries him to his death in a hopeless raid. He sleeps in the midst of a raid now without lance or enemies, death needs only the icy wind and the snow that falls on the last Tehuelches, tiny dots in the middle of the Pampas, animals without firewood or food; the last heretics from the plain full of rocks.

(Lago Blanco, Chubut, in memory of Manuel Quilchamal)

POLVO MOJADO

Una tras otra, las playas abandonadas por aquello que la civilización llama turismo contienen lo elemental para vivir o morir de hambre. Variadas maneras de enfrentar lo inevitable, la soledad, bajo las mareas que sacuden la seguridad, el confort que no existe sobre la arena pelada, polvo mojado que traerá desazón para los débiles, orgullo para quienes sean capaces de oler el poniente sin más fe que su propia cáscara. Lejos del Trópico, las manos del agua imponen respeto y furor por la luna nueva, los roqueríos donde anida el pájaro que alcanzará a vernos morir, la inevitable sonoridad del grillo que anuncia gracia y sobrevivirá a la tempestad. No vendrán ladrones hasta aquí, serían devorados por la desesperación, pero estamos nosotros, ladrones de fuego escaldados por el incendio de las ciudades. Seremos robados por nuestra propia pasión.

(Playa Magagna, en casa del poeta Ankudovich)

WET DUST

One after another, the beaches abandoned by what civilization calls tourism contain all that's needed to live or die of hunger. Various ways of confronting the inevitable, the solitude, under the high seas that shake security, the comfort that doesn't exist on the bald sand, wet dust that unsettles the weak, pride for those who're able to smell the west wind with no faith but their own hide. Far from the Tropic, watery hands impose respect and fury for the new moon, the rocks with the nest of the bird that will get to see us die, the inevitable music of the cricket that announces grace and will survive the storm. No thieves will come this far, they'd be devoured by despair, but we're here, stealing fire and scalded by the razing of the cities. We'll be robbed by our own passion.

(Playa Magagna, Chubut, in the house of the poet Ankudovich)

SUFRIR, SIN LLORAR

En una estación de ómnibus hecha para no durar ni ser vista, he visto huir a quienes abandonan todo, derrotados por la miseria más que por la inmensidad. Vuelven al norte final, origen de la primera pobreza antes de que hallaran ésta, bajo otro nombre. Dejan casas alineadas morosamente en barrios oscuros, sin revocar, peladas de todo verde, y un enorme monumento blanquecino, de fealdad soviética. Pierden el empleo y el interés, y la esperanza del progreso, que consistía en pasar noches eternas en la boca de los pozos de petróleo, helados y borrachos, perseverando en el cuidado frenético de la riqueza ajena. Las luces del alba descubrieron el puerto de aguas grises, furiosas en medio del invierno, a espaldas de cualquier viaje. Sufrí, pero no lloré, atento a tanta caída propia y ajena, con la compasión de quien no sabe regresar ni partir a tiempo.

(Caleta Olivia)

SUFFER, WITHOUT WEEPING

In a bus station built not to last or be seen, I've seen them fleeing, abandoning everything, defeated by misery more than immensity. They return to the final north, source of their first poverty before they found this one, under another name. They leave in default houses lined up in dark neighbourhoods, unfinished, shorn of all green, an enormous, blanching monument, of soviet ugliness. They lose work and interest, and the hope of progress, which consisted of spending eternal nights at the mouth of the oil wells, frozen and drunk, dedicated to the frenzied care of someone else's wealth. The dawn lights uncover the port with its grey waters, furious in the middle of winter, back turned to any journey. I suffered, but didn't weep, attentive to so many falls, my own and others', with the compassion of one who doesn't know how to return or leave on time.

(Caleta Olivia, Santa Cruz)

NO HAY AFUERA

Una caja metálica lanzada al camino construye un mundo. El alrededor pende de una cuerda mental. La lógica de los sonidos late con el motor que aúlla en el largo desierto humano. No hay afuera mientras se viaja, una charca de destellos es el futuro y una imagen distorsionada por los espejos lo que dejamos atrás sin remordernos. Aparte de lo que sucede en la jaula de vidrios, sólo el camino desconocido posee fuerza de encanto. La vida del universo tiene a ese viaje como único sostén.

(La Pedrera)

THERE'S NO OUTSIDE

A metal box launched onto the road builds a world. The surroundings hang from a mental thread. The logic of the sounds beats with the motor that howls in the long human desert. There's no outside when you travel, a pool of sparks is the future and an image distorted by mirrors is what we leave behind without regret. Outside what happens in the glass cage, only the unknown road has the power to charm. The life of the universe depends on nothing but that journey.

(La Pedrera, Uruguay)

LA MAGNÍFICA SOLEDAD

Un balcón asoma al frío del Atlántico, donde la soledad es magnífica y desesperante. La luz amarilla del faro ilumina cada diez o doce segundos la costa, para orientar a los buques que nunca han de llegar. El canto rodado, vacío de pisadas durante siglos, dibuja un semicírculo perfecto como contorno del agua que viene a pulir los restos de una vida. Sometidos por el estruendo, dos hombres que cargan armas inútiles toman nota de los barcos que imaginan en el horizonte. Ocho sepulcros blanquean al pie del promontorio ocre. Un corral de metal negro rodea a una de las fosas cubiertas de piedras, distinción para otro muerto desconocido en un territorio donde apenas son célebres los asesinos. Ningún nombre designa a estos huesos, ningún desafío al olvido que hubiera llegado de cualquier manera, por acumulación o por impacto.

(Cabo Blanco)

THE MAGNIFICENT SOLITUDE

A headland peeks out into the cold of the Atlantic, where the solitude is magnificent and desperate. The yellow beam of the lighthouse illuminates the coast every ten or twelve seconds, to guide the ships that must never arrive. The pebble beach, empty of footsteps for centuries, draws a perfect semicircle like an outline of the water that comes to polish the remains of a life. Subdued by the din, two men carrying useless weapons take note of the boats they imagine on the horizon. Eight sepulchres blanche at the foot of the ochre headland. A black metal barrier surrounds one of the graves covered with stones, a distinction for another of the unknown dead in a territory where only murderers are famous. No name denotes these bones, no challenge to the oblivion that would have arrived anyway, by accumulation or by impact.

(Cabo Blanco, Santa Cruz)

DE ENFERMEDAD O DE HAMBRE

El buzón de correos interrumpe la monotonía de la meseta, erguido junto al edificio amarillento que han decorado con piedras lajas. En leguas a la redonda no queda una casa en pie. Nadie está para escribir una carta, o los sobres carecen de destinatorios, para qué abriría alguien esta puerta. Los muebles tienen la apariencia de haber sido abandonados con las llaves puestas, las casillas vacías y un sobre nunca reclamado que asoma bajo el polvo. Una liebre ha entrado quién sabe cómo en la oficina de atención al público, y ha muerto allí, de enfermedad o de hambre. Unos cueros de oveja cubren el cerco metálico, y los grandes eucaliptus simulan un lied con el paso de los vientos.

(Nueva Lübecka)

OF ILLNESS OR OF HUNGER

The post-office box interrupts the monotony of the plateau, erect next to the yellowing building they've decorated with sandstone. For leagues around there's not a house left standing. There's no one to write a letter, or the envelopes lack addressees, why would anyone open this door. The furniture looks like it's been abandoned with the keys in the door, the pigeonholes empty and an unclaimed envelope that pokes out under the dust. A hare has somehow got behind the customer service desk, and has died there, of illness or of hunger. Some sheepskins cover the metallic grille, and the big eucalyptus trees feign a lied with the passing of the winds.

(Nueva Lübecka, Chubut)

EL ESPÍRITU DE LOS PEONES

La ilusión da tumbos, se hunde cada tarde en el mar como los pájaros gordos y pesados que revolotean en el barracón. Los nadadores se zambullen entre las sobras del puerto y el sol mortecino rebota sobre el alambre de cobre con que atan sus pantalones. La ilusión es una hamaca sobre el abismo que cubre la arena de las playas, no es nada que pueda dibujarse sobre un papel de estraza. La ilusión no cabalga sobre este mar tampoco, jadea sobre las caderas de las mujeres que calientan el polvo del desierto y lo hacen música entre la pobreza. Los barcos brillan en óxido y alcohol, se recortan sobre el puerto vacío de salitre, las mujeres del norte se dejan poseer por el espíritu de los peones muertos, se dejan tumbar sobre una maldición, son espejos que no han de reflejar otra cosa, ojos mirando al cielo como si la oscuridad y la sinrazón fueran a reinar por siempre.

(Antofagasta)

THE SPIRIT OF THE PEONS

Illusion stumbles, it sinks each evening in the sea like the fat, heavy birds that whirl about in the billet. The swimmers dive in the port's leftovers and the dying sun rebounds off the copper wire they use to tie up their trousers. Illusion is a swing over the abyss that the beach sand covers, it's nothing that could be drawn on rough paper. Illusion rides no horse on this sea either, it breathes heavy on the hips of the women who warm the dust of the desert and turn it to music amid the poverty. The boats shine in rust and alcohol, cut out against the port empty of saltpetre, the women from the north let themselves be taken by the spirit of the dead peons, be tumbled on a curse, they're mirrors that mustn't reflect anything else, eyes looking at the sky as if darkness and unreason were to reign forever.

(Antofagasta, Chile)[8]

LA OVEJA

¿Levantar la cabeza?
¿Dónde cree que estamos, en la Patagonia?

Samuel Beckett

Atrapada por el cuello al alambre de púas, un mal movimiento
la degollaría. La oveja desliza milímetros su cabeza hasta quedar
inmóvil a la espera de una solución que escapa a sus propios
movimientos. Su cabeza no piensa, ni esboza cursos de acción,
apenas percibe el suave ardor de los alambres puntiagudos,
mientras a unos metros del alambrado los vehículos atraviesan
la soledad. Pasan sin verla, o ven apenas la imagen fugaz de una
oveja que permanece muy cerca de la ruta, en una inmovilidad sólo
rota por gestos imperceptibles. Atrapada por el cuello al alambre
de púas, oye la secuencia creciente y luego decreciente de los
motores, quieta se queda y algo semejante al placer percibe cuando
logra la quietud absoluta. Empieza a dolerle cuando se adormece,
y así se despierta, y vuelven a nublarse sus ojos azules hasta que
regresa el dolor que para ella no tiene nombre. No puede estimar la
duración de la noche ni aspira al azar de alguien que atine a separar
su cabeza del alambre.

THE SHEEP

Raise his head?
Where do you think we are? In Patagonia?

Samuel Beckett

Trapped by the neck on the barbed wire, a mistaken movement would slit her throat. The sheep slides her head millimetres until she's motionless awaiting a solution that escapes her own movements. Her head doesn't think, nor sketch courses of action, she scarcely perceives the smooth warmth of the pointed wires, meanwhile a few metres from the fencing the vehicles cross the solitude. They pass without seeing her, or see just the fleeting image of a sheep that stays very close to the road, in an immobility only broken by imperceptible gestures. Trapped by the neck on the barbed wire, she hears the sequence, rising and then falling, of the motors, silent she stays and perceives something close to pleasure when she achieves absolute quietude. It starts to hurt her when she dozes, and so she wakes up, and again her blue eyes cloud over until the return of the pain for which she has no name. She cannot guess the duration of the night nor hold on to the hope of a hand that would help separate her head from the wire.

PART TWO

The Foreign Passion (Revised and Expanded)
European and African Travels

> ...*there are still songs to sing beyond*
> *mankind*
> Paul Celan
> (trans. Paul Joris)

Where can it be found again,
An elsewhere world, beyond
Maps and atlases,
Where all is woven into
And of itself, like a nest
Of crosshatched grass blades?

Seamus Heaney

> *The class struggle ...*
> *is a struggle for the rough*
> *and material things, without*
> *which there is nothing*
> *fine and spiritual.*
> Walter Benjamin
> (trans. Dennis Redmond)

How ought such a natural
history of destruction to begin?

W. G. Sebald
(trans. Anthea Bell)

Six million ways to die, choose one: drugs, depression, destitution.
So many forms of catatonic collapse. In earlier times, 'deviants,
psychotics and the mentally collapsed' inspired militant-poets,
situationists, rave-dreamers. Now they are incarcerated in hospitals,
or languishing in the gutter.

Mark Fisher

LOS DIENTES DEL PAPA

Inspirado en Francis Bacon

Los perros desorbitados, famélicos, muerden desde su centro atroz, giran sin detenerse bajo el foco de la maldad del mundo. Inocentes en su furia, contrastados con la luz violenta de la mirada humana, sus dentelladas acusan al matador, al verdadero demiurgo de su propia violencia. Tras las paredes que sostienen la imagen, perros idénticos de otra realidad persiguen a un borracho enloquecido por la intemperie. Ellos son una conciencia del mundo que merecería no existir. Aun así muerden menos que los dientes del Papa, que Bacon dejó para recordarnos el infierno, la otra cara del cielo redentor en la tierra. Ése tiene mandíbulas afiladas en la carne de hombres de fe insuficiente, apóstatas, magas, científicos, amantes de todos los signos, pederastas sin sotana y otras especies ajenas a la compasión de un dios. Hay una profesión de fe en la encía que brilla con dientes de Inquisición y recuerdos de la miseria católica.

(Galería Hugh Lane, Dublin)

THE POPE'S TEETH

Inspired by Francis Bacon

The wide-eyed, famished dogs gnash out from their atrocious centre, spin ceaselessly under the spotlight of the world's malice. Innocent in their fury, set against the violent light of the human gaze, their teeth-marks accuse the killer, the true creator of his own violence. The other side of the walls holding up the image, identical dogs from another reality chase a drunkard sent mad by exposure. They are a conscience of a world that deserves not to exist. Even so, they bite less than the Pope's teeth, which Bacon left us as a reminder of hell, the other face of the redemptive heaven on earth. That one has jaws sharpened on the flesh of men of little faith, apostates, witches, scientists, lovers of every stripe, cassock-less pederasts and other species beyond god's compassion. There is a profession of faith in the gums that gleam with inquisitor's teeth and memories of Catholic misery.

(Hugh Lane Gallery, Dublin)

LA SENDA IDÉNTICA

El pastor trashuma entre alambradas de púas eléctricas, basurales humeantes y grúas Caterpillar. Guía a sus ovejas de nuevo siglo para esquivar el vertido de las fábricas, les impide beber de eso, aunque estas bestias omnívoras tragan casi sin masticar todo lo que encuentran a su paso. Ni siquiera, piensa el pastor mientras las conduce con la ayuda del perro flaco, fruncen su nariz al percibir el olor que asemeja al de una pila de muertos. Recorren una senda antigua, de cuando la dehesa ocupaba esta tierra y las naves industriales no existían. Sabe sin embargo que su padre y su abuelo hicieron lo mismo. El aire era fresco y puro, pero la senda iba, igual que ahora, desde el pie del cerro hasta la cumbre donde viven los dueños. El castillo iluminado por luces potentes es el mismo que miró su abuelo en esa subida de esclavos, bordeando el camino. Su miseria es la misma. Todo ha atravesado los siglos en la misma dirección prevista.

(Consuegra)

THE IDENTICAL PATH

The shepherd drives his flock between electrified barbed wire, steaming rubbish tips and Caterpillar cranes. He guides his twenty-first-century sheep around factory waste, he stops them drinking that, although these omnivore beasts gulp down anything they find on their path. They don't even, thinks the shepherd while he moves them with the help of a skinny dog, turn their noses up at the smell, like what a pile of dead bodies gives off. They follow an ancient path, from when these lands were meadows and the warehouses didn't exist. He knows, though, that his father and his grandfather did the same. The air was fresh and pure, but the path went, just as it does now, from the foot of the hill to the summit, where the owners live. The castle, lit up by powerful lights, is the same one his grandfather saw in that slave's climb, alongside the path. His poverty is the same. Everything has crossed the centuries in the same, predictable direction.

(Consuegra, Spain)

LA SIESTA DE LOS VIVOS

La misa a la que asisten con unción los viejos es rutinaria, aunque
los vitrales tamizan una luz que atraviesa sus cabezas, y el fresco
algo mohoso de la catedral alivia su espíritu en el mediodía del
verano. Salen reconfortados o tranquilos, y se acumulan frente
a la lista clavada en el mural exterior de la iglesia. Miran con
detenimiento y congoja real, aunque controlada, el nombre de
los muertos del pueblo en la última semana, que el párroco ha
escrito con letra menuda y una cruz pequeña junto a cada apellido.
Comentan detalles de los muertos más cercanos, comparan edades,
describen el estado aproximado en que se encontraban en los días
últimos, sacuden la cabeza o disimulan la mueca. Después, parten
con una sonrisa hacia el sol, el fresco, el cocido que sabrá mejor
después del regreso, pensando en el tinto de verano y en la siesta
de los vivos. La fe de la celebración se hace notar en su semblante,
la otra vida prometida es ésta.

(El Toboso)

THE SLEEP OF THE LIVING

The mass the living devotedly attend is run-of-the-mill, though the stained-glass filters a light that cuts through their heads, and the rather mouldy cool of the cathedral lightens their spirits on this summer's midday. They leave reassured or calm, and gather in front of the list pinned to the outer wall of the church. They look carefully, with real – but controlled – anguish, at the names of those who've died in the town that last week, which the priest has written in small letters with a little cross next to each surname. They chat about the dead closest to them, compare ages, describe what sort of state they were in those last days, shake their heads or mask a grimace. Then, they leave, smiling towards the sun, the cool air, the stew that will taste better on their return, thinking about the summer wine and the sleep of the living. The sacrament's faith is written on their faces, the promised other life is this.

(El Toboso, Spain)

UNOS TALLOS FLACOS

Estos molinos se mueven con el viento, pero no son para batirse a duelo. El Quijote ha sido confinado a las escuelas. Llevan la electricidad lejos de aquí, me dice el viejo de barba dura y cigarro grueso. Nosotros no luchamos con esos molinos, ríe, pero nos alumbramos a keroseno como mi padre. Unos tallos flacos, aunque erguidos como el viejo, resisten a la sequía. Él masca un rábano, ofrece su vino áspero de la tierra en un vaso de terracota y se limita a no esperar nada. Así nadie sufre la impaciencia, dice. Carajo, dice.

(La Hiruela)

SOME THIN STALKS

These windmills move in the breeze, but they are not to be tilted at. Don Quixote has been confined to schools. They take electricity far from here, says the old man with his wiry beard and thick cigar. We don't fight those windmills, he laughs, but we still burn kerosene for light like my father did. Some thin stalks, though like the old man still standing, resist the drought. He chews a radish, offers his bitter wine from this soil in a terracotta cup and does no more than wait for nothing. So no one suffers impatience, he says. God damn it, he says.

(La Hiruela, Spain)

ARMAS LARGAS INOCENTES

Los niños disparan unas armas largas inocentes aquí. Es un juego de guerra simulado en una pantalla, y sus cabezas aprenden el significado de las herramientas antes que el de las palabras. Escenas precisas recrean victorias. El tigre reproducido con la angustia de recibir el balazo en la frente se convierte en receptor humano del mismo proyectil, según la sala. Los caídos constituyen la causa necesaria, el reverso imaginado de la colección de armas de la historia. Cuando el visitante descolocado se revuelve en la duda y enfila la salida, una pequeña sala recrea Afganistán.

(Museo de la Armería Real, Leeds)

INNOCENT RIFLES

Children can fire innocent rifles here. It's a war simulation on the screen, and their minds learn the meaning of the tools before the words. Precise scenes recreate victories. The tiger depicted in pain, taking a bullet between the eyes, turns into a human recipient of the same projectile, depending on the room. The fallen provide the necessary cause, the imaginary flipside to the collection of historical weapons. As the disorientated visitor goes over his doubts and heads for the exit, a little room recreates Afghanistan.

(Royal Armouries Museum, Leeds)

EL QUE TOSE PARA ADENTRO

*La lenta cancelación del futuro comenzó en las décadas de 1970
y 1980. Nunca seré capaz de vivir según la nueva realidad, sin
importar cuán evidente, inconfundible o incluso encandiladora
sea a escala planetaria.*

Franco 'Bifo' Berardi

Un bar cerrado a cal y canto a la gracia del día. Se bebe, sí, pero
no es ésa la ocupación que aquí se cultiva más. El que ve pasar
el mundo, abandonado tras las ventanas desnortadas de cualquier
éxito, el que tose para adentro su pudor o fracaso, el que grita para
decir que tiene sonidos todavía, el que desafía a los presentes pero
sobre todo a los muertos, y después se refugia en la herida más
cruel para no hablar más hasta la hora del cierre. El bar no abre las
ventanas ni ventila el alma jamás, los caídos no dejan de llegar, y
no quieren ver la calle en que se golpearon. Vamos a un ritmo aquí,
no hay semana ni lunes que nos destroce del todo como afuera.
Aquí se sueña con morir, las hazañas jamás son verdaderas pero
perduran; se vive con lo que no se tiene. La esperanza no es otra
cosa que una ronda más, pagada por otro.

(Pub The Eldon, Leeds)

THE MAN WHO COUGHS DOWN

*The slow cancellation of the future got underway in the 1970s
and 80s. I'll never be able to live in accordance with the new
reality, no matter how evident, unmistakable, or even dazzling its
social planetary trends.*

Franco 'Bifo' Berardi

A bar bricked shut to the joys of the day. Drinking, yes there's
drinking, but that's not the real work here. One man watching the
world go by, abandoned behind the windows with no compass to
success, another who coughs down his shame or failure, or another
who shouts to say that he can still make a sound, or who calls out
everyone present but above all the dead, and then hides away in the
cruellest wound to avoid speaking until closing time. The bar never
opens its windows and never airs the soul, the fallen keep arriving,
and don't want to see the street where they beat each other up.
We've got a rhythm going here, there's no week or Monday that
destroys us as completely as outside. Here you dream about dying,
the boasts are never true but they last; you live with what you don't
have. Hope is just another round that someone else is buying.

(The Eldon, Leeds)

BAJO EL PUÑO CERRADO

La anciana reposa insomne al borde de la ventana y oye el susurro de que, todavía, es posible amanecer. Aferra un objeto que bajo el puño cerrado asoma como objeto religioso, reliquia o pañuelo oscuro. A pocos metros de su puerta patrullan soldados que pueden provenir de un imperio cercano o de otra galaxia; es lo mismo para su conciencia o su memoria del dolor. Ellos marcan la línea del alba. Mientras, sin guía ni legado, un país existe, se crea de nuevo, sobrevive por razones ajenas a las que presenta la historia. Las razones para morir como héroes o mártires, los argumentos para matar a unas órdenes conocidas por motivos desconocidos, fueron una oración al destino.

(Enniskillen)

UNDER HER CLENCHED FIST

The old lady rests sleepless by the side of the window and listens to the whispering hint of a still possible dawn. She holds on to something that under her clenched fist pokes out like a religious object, a relic or a dark handkerchief. A few yards from her door soldiers patrol, from a nearby empire or another galaxy, perhaps; it's all the same for her conscience or memory of pain.[9] They mark the line of daybreak. Meanwhile, with no guide or legacy, a country exists, it's made again, survives for reasons other than those offered by history.[10] The reasons for dying like heroes or martyrs, the arguments for killing on known orders for unknown motives, were a prayer to destiny.

(Enniskillen)

EL NIÑO QUE RÍE

Todo está en este sitio, todo lo pasado ya, tanto, imposible de recordar. Sobre la calle Falls un niño corre en sandalias con el pan. Ríe levemente, como si la libertad fuera este silencio, la mañana rutinaria, la madre que lo espera para servir la mesa. Decenas de muertos a una edad ligeramente superior a la suya lo contemplan desde las paredes que nadie parece atreverse a sepultar con cal. Como la memoria de la primera infancia, sus olores, esas pinturas se graban en la mente del niño que corre. Él corre a casa, y está abierta la puerta, y en el íntimo jardín delantero se acumulan sus juguetes, unas flores de plástico, y están pegados sus dibujos en la ventana. Cuánto vale esta paz opaca, sus sandalias sonando sobre el asfalto desparejo, cómo describirá la dignidad este niño cuando crezca, cuando se pregunte por los muertos de las paredes, el silencio, el dolor en sordina de los vecinos.

(Belfast)

THE LAUGHING CHILD

Everything can be found here, everything past now, so much, impossible to recall. On the Falls Road a child in sandals runs carrying bread. He laughs softly, as if freedom were this silence, the routine morning, the mother waiting for him before she serves up. Dozens of dead, at an age just a touch older than his, watch him from walls that no one dares to bury with quicklime. Like the memory of early infancy, its smells, these pictures are engraved in the mind of the running child. He runs home, and the door is open, and in the little front garden are piled up his toys, some plastic flowers, and his drawings are stuck to the wall. What price this dark peace, his sandals flapping on the uneven tarmac, how will he describe this dignity when he's grown up, when he asks himself about the dead on the walls, the silence, the mute pain of his neighbours.

(Belfast)

A LAS LLAMAS

Algo proviene de ese fondo oscuro de convicción y sangre, corazón y miembros rotos, órganos estallados. Alguna cosa íntima que no puede reducirse a lonjas de lugar común. 'Fanáticos', 'los asesinos', 'los desviados'. Manchan como hojarasca las palabras, dichas con soberbia moral, la miseria del léxico. Algo surge de un fondo, lo increado, tiempos de fango, sumisión y piedra arrastrada cien veces hasta el agotamiento de la humillación. Necesidad de expiación, nada religioso, un Alarico que se consume en su propio fuego. No se pide perdón o misericordia, por dignidad. Cada uno se entrega a las llamas con la santidad oscura de quien traga su propia historia.

(Strabane)

TO THE FLAMES

Something comes out of those dark depths of conviction and blood, heart and broken limbs, exploded organs. Something private that can't be reduced to slices of cliché. 'Fanatics', 'murderers', 'perverts'. Said with moral superiority, words stain like leaf-fall, the poverty of the lexicon. Something comes up from the deep, the uncreated, times of slime, submission and a rock dragged a hundred times until the humiliation runs out. The need to atone, nothing religious, a King Alaric consumed in his own flames. No pardon or mercy is asked, for dignity's sake. Each one gives himself to the flames with the dark sanctity of one swallowing his own history.

(Strabane, County Tyrone)

LA NAVAJA DEL DESCUBRIDOR

Marcados por la navaja del descubridor y el cilicio del sacerdote, choznos o nietos de ellos mismos, criminales por herencia, regresamos desde el borde de la miseria a pisar su tierra. Herejes abandonados a sus textos sublimes, aprendimos a escribir leyendo libros de los que abominamos, con una admiración llamada rencor. Sólo al llegar, nosotros les recordamos que su hambre antigua y su voracidad viajaron antes desde este continente rancio hacia nuestros países lejanos de verdor, sangre y minerales. Por eso se odian en nosotros.

(Valladolid)

THE CONQUISTADOR'S BLADE

Marked by the conquistador's blade or the priest's sackcloth, their very distant heirs, criminals by inheritance, we return from the edge of despair to tread their lands. Heretics abandoned to their sublime texts, we learnt to write reading books by those we abhor, with an admiration called rancour. But when we arrive, we remind them that their ancient hunger and voraciousness travelled before from this ancient continent to our distant countries of pasture, blood and minerals. That's why they hate themselves in us.

(Valladolid, Spain)

UN MAR SIN AGUA

Sólo se puede hablar de justicia en los libros sagrados, ésos, escritos a sangre y fuego con una lengua uniforme que aspira a volverse única. Los enemigos de la fe mueren siempre justamente; de cada fe, un verdugo. Para qué dios calma o detiene la herida del niño pronto a morir para que muera apenas más tarde, la sangre del padre ausente para siempre, el fusilado sin culpa. Hablar de lo justo es hablar de lo inexistente, de un mar sin agua donde nos ahogamos. Pero se trata de aquello que merecemos, horca o destino. Las nubes pasan sobre una humanidad que llora, agoniza y al mirar al cielo sólo ve esos cúmulos de aire y tormenta. Todos merecen un destino que les será arrebatado, ningún horizonte es suficiente para el que va a morir ahora de soledad y rabia, y espera disparos sobre el cuerpo de todo el mundo.

(Canterbury)

A SEA WITHOUT WATER

One can only speak of justice in sacred texts, yes those, written in blood and fire with a uniform language that aspires to be the only one. The enemies of faith die justly, always; for each faith, an executioner. Why does God calm or stanch the wound of the child about to die for him to die a few moments later, the blood of the father absent for ever, the man shot without guilt. To speak of what's just is to speak of the non-existent, of a sea without water where we drown. But it's about what we deserve, gallows or destiny. Clouds pass over a humanity that weeps, dies and looking at the sky sees only those cumuli of air and storms. Everyone deserves a destiny that will be snatched from them, no horizon is enough for someone who'll die now of solitude and rage, and awaits shots fired over the body of everyone.

(Canterbury, Kent)

NUESTRAS HERRAMIENTAS

Tanteamos siglos en lo oscuro. Sin embargo queda un brillo mínimo allá, en lo hondo, que cada uno rastrea con los instrumentos que le quedan. Pedernal, afiladores de concha marina, palo de santo, pequeños cuchillos, lanzadores, huesos delicados de animales, grasa, punzones, maza de roble, dagas o cuchillos de mesa bruñidos por la vanguardia, cueros suaves, mordillos. Usamos hasta la extenuación los dientes para bruñir los vidrios opacos que dificultan el paso de la luz. Nunca son suficientes nuestras herramientas. Pero esa luz, así, corta los acantilados a pique y alcanza a revelarse contra el fondo siempre oscuro de la iniquidad, el habla de los dioses que la amparan siempre, brilla contra la consagración de sus ejecutores.

(Glamorgan)

OUR TOOLS

We fumble about for centuries in the dark. Yet there's still a bare glow there, in the depths, that each one of us tracks with the instruments available. Flint, seashell sharpeners, *palo santo*, little daggers, throwing knives, delicate animal bones, fat, stamps, an oak mace, stilettos or table knives burnished by the vanguard, smooth leathers, teething rings. We wear out our teeth polishing the dark glass that blocks the passage of light. Our tools are never enough. But that light, like that, cuts the cliffs at an angle, just enough to be seen against the ever-dark background of iniquity (always helped by the speech of the gods), to shine against the consecration of its executioners.

(Glamorgan)

LA DESTRUCCIÓN PERMANECE

Las piedras, una sobre otra, decenas de miles en cada muro casi derrumbado. No se ve el movimiento de manos numerosas, apremiadas, carcomidas mucho antes que el muro. El pueblo sigue siendo morada, mientras la destrucción permanece. En este día resulta difícil descubrir el rastro de los vivos, la memoria del mismo Adriano, pero ahí están, enmudecidos, a la buena de sí mismos que no de dios. La piedra dura y dura, la piedra sobre otra piedra, aquí se edificó el olvido, una casa fría, el recinto para los animales a la entrada. La piedra abandonada es cobijo inerte, piedra de abandono. Detrás de cada fragmento del Imperio un ser casi desquiciado asoma su rostro con desconfianza, hace el gesto de visera con su mano, se refugia detrás de ella como protección inútil. Ha visto derruirse estos muros que parecían eternos, y teme que algo más caiga sobre su cabeza.

(Greenhead)

THE DESTRUCTION REMAINS

The stones, one atop the other, tens of thousands in each barely-standing wall. No one sees the movement of many hands, hurried, worn away long before the wall. The town is still inhabited, while the destruction remains. On this day it's difficult to find the trace of the living, the memory of Hadrian himself, but they're there, fallen mute, by the will of themselves if not of God. The stone lasts and lasts, stone on another stone, here was built forgetting, a cold house, the space for animals by the door. Abandoned stone is inert shelter, stone of abandonment. Behind every fragment of the Empire someone half-unhinged pokes their head out untrustingly, shields their eyes with their hand, takes refuge behind it like useless protection. They've seen these walls collapse though they seemed eternal, and fear something else falling on their heads.

(Greenhead, Northumberland)

ROSTROS EN EL METRO

Para Concha García

Mezclados en la raza de Babel, es muy tarde para ser, en cualquier sentido, los únicos. Los policías persiguen por olor, raza, procedencia, mientras su humanidad sorda se aniquila. Cómo salir del campo negro de las fronteras, si venimos de África, sur América, de toda la tierra final que antes fue descubierta y cartografiada para ser dada a la inteligencia de los ilustrados. Traemos deudas para cobrar a los dueños de la Aduana que nos confisca el Nombre. Venimos a empujar el carro mortuorio de la Europa anciana que nos amonesta. Somos vándalos, dicen, que pisamos el ágora con nuestros trastos, y empujamos malamente hacia el abismo la silla de muertos que rueda con sus cuerpos blancos y medievales. Persigue rostros en el Metro la recaída Europa.

(Barcelona)

FACES ON THE METRO

For Concha García

Mixed up with the Babel race, it's too late to be, in any sense, unique. The police track by smell, race, origin, while their deaf humanity is rubbed out. How can we leave the black sites of borders, if we come from Africa, South America, all those endlands that first were discovered and mapped to be handed over to the intelligence of the enlightened. We come with debts to collect from the owners of the Customs House that confiscates our Name. We come to push the bier of old Europe even as it admonishes us. We're the vandals, they say, who crowd the Agora with our junk, and clumsily shove into the abyss the deathchair that rolls with its white, medieval bodies. Chasing faces on the Metro, Europe in relapse.

(Barcelona)

EL HÉROE SUSPENDIDO

Una iglesia que flota en la eternidad de la piedra rota. Un Cristo cuelga de la galería central, descentrado del altar, y provoca pavor contemplarlo desde abajo. Siempre estamos sujetos a algo que flota sobre nosotros, deidad, lluvia o desgracia. O se trata de un ser superior a fuerza de repeticiones, convertido en dios con escrituras reescritas hasta resistir la borradura. Caen gotas del techo sobre este suspendido eterno, callado en su diálogo con un padre presunto, que no es criminal sino negligente. La belleza del órgano en las alturas, las piedras alineadas en el siglo XV, la sensación climática, espiritual, de quien llega en busca del fresco durante una caminata de verano y musita "gracias, señor". La belleza del encofrado, una disposición original de las maderas del techo, el trabajo silencioso acumulado por generaciones de sirvientes que cargaron los tributos de los creyentes antiguos, todo eso se ve en la iglesia desierta. No hay reino, pero nos sentimos muy abajo, aplastados por la fuerza magnética del héroe suspendido.

(St. David's)

THE SUSPENDED HERO

A church that floats in the eternity of broken stone. A Christ hangs in the central gallery, off-centred from the altar, and contemplating it from below fills you with fear. We are always subject to something that floats above us, deity, rainfall, or misfortune. Or a being made superior by force of repetition, turned into a god with scriptures rewritten until they resist erasure. Droplets fall from the roof onto the eternally suspended one, silent in his dialogue with a supposed father, who is not criminal but negligent. The beauty of the organ up high, the stones aligned in the fifteenth century, the sensation – climatic, spiritual – when you've come in search of cool air on a summer walk and mutter, "thank you, Lord". The beauty of the coffering, an original layout for the beams of the ceiling, the silent work accumulated by generations of servants who carried the tributes of the ancient faithful, all that is on display in the deserted church. There is no kingdom, but we feel like we're right down low, crushed by the magnetic force of the suspended hero.

(St. David's, Pembrokeshire)

SANTOS DE RELIGIÓN NINGUNA

Inspirado en los Alabaster heads, de Jaume Plensa

Las cabezas corroídas, cada una de modo único, atormentadas que sonríen o amagan con hacerlo sin concretarlo nunca. Cada una tiene una perspectiva de integridad que permite obviar cómo ese monstruo indetenible – el tiempo, la preparación del crimen – los va carcomiendo. Hay ácidos debajo de nuestro cuerpo, y, cuando alcanzamos a pensarlo, el daño ya nos ha quitado partes esenciales de nosotros. Hay una luz purísima que los hace santos de religión ninguna: brillan así aún con la llama de lo destruido en cada cabeza. La destrucción parcial o total de nuestros cuerpos no podrá con la belleza o armonía que cargamos, incluso a pesar de nuestras mentes de alabastro.

(Parque de Esculturas de Yorkshire)

SAINTS OF NO RELIGION

Inspired by Jaume Plensa's Alabaster Heads

The heads corroded, each in its own way, like torture victims who smile, or threaten to, without ever getting there. Each one sees with such integrity that they can overlook the way the unstoppable monster – time, the planning of a crime – gnaws away at them. There are acids beneath our body and, by the time we realise, the damage has already stripped away essential parts of us. There's the purest of lights that makes them saints of no religion: they shine like that even with the flame of what's destroyed on each head. The partial or total destruction of our bodies is no match for the beauty or harmony we carry, even in spite of our alabaster minds.

(Yorkshire Sculpture Park)

HUDSON REGRESA A INGLATERRA

Para Carlos Gamerro

En memoria de William Henry Hudson

Hudson viaja en bicicleta por las islas mientras recuerda caballos jadeantes de la pampa aquella. Lleva polainas y atuendo raído, y su mirada resplandece del infinito que pudo ver. Tiene un sombrero que ha traído desde aquel país lejano donde supo renacer para ver lo incógnito, y recorre siempre ese límite desdibujado por Borges entre la pampa e Inglaterra. Del otro lado del Atlántico quedó una casa donde aprendió a percibir algún dios en el olor de los animales y el andar huidizo de pájaros y gauchos. En su inglés matizado con palabras de peones y matreros maldice a su suerte y a su regreso. Aquí hace lo mismo que allá, en los confines, pero el horizonte inglés lo viene ahogando. El diálogo incesante con los pájaros, esos bichos que detienen el tiempo, le dio días de ocio y un ritmo celestial que desnuda hasta lo que permanece bajo el paisaje. Él mismo es tratado como pájaro desplumado, aunque vuela con aires de otra especie.

(Broadwater)

HUDSON RETURNS TO ENGLAND

For Carlos Gamerro

In memory of William Henry Hudson

Hudson bicycles around the islands, remembering panting horses away on the Pampas. He wears gaiters and frayed clothes, and his gaze shines with the infinite horizon he could see there. He has a hat he brought from that distant country where he was reborn to see the unknown, and he travels always along the edge of that line, which Borges blurred, between the Pampas and England. On the other side of the Atlantic there's still a house where he learnt to feel a godlike presence in the smell of animals and the fleeting movement of birds and gauchos. In his English, nuanced with words from peons and bandits, he curses his luck and his return. Here he does just what he did there, on the margins, but the English horizon steadily chokes him. The ceaseless conversation with the birds, those creatures who stop time, gave him days of leisure and a celestial rhythm that strips even what remains beneath the landscape. He's treated like a plucked bird, though he flies with airs of another species.

(Broadwater, West Sussex)

RESISTENCIA

Los comunistas guardaban sueños,
los comunistas, los comunistas.

Caetano Veloso

Para Jorge Boccanera

La izquierda no llega, no alcanza la izquierda, no ve el final la travestida. No ve nada, ni el final de la miseria ni su principio. La derecha come de todo, todo es derecha en este mundo, una mandíbula ciega que tritura, calma para tragarse las víctimas y cobrar por la eternidad la sumisión o voto desconcertado. Las almitas engañadas por la instrucción cívica de las democracias van aderezadas rumbo a esa dentadura de ónix. No podrás levantar muros ni alambradas en tan feroz estómago. Cuando la tiranía es un sangrado diario que opera por goteo y viene con el agua de las cloacas en envase certificado de residuos nucleares, la resistencia es susurro, oración pagana, una bomba de detonación que llega en viaje desde una guerra pasada, el recuerdo de Marx que cura todos los desvaríos pero nos deja en Siberia o en un estante de la biblioteca. El capital acumulado en sangre es legal, mortal, eterno en las manos de siempre. El Capital debe ser leído como un Sutra. Todo trabajo es forzado.

(Biblioteca Chetham, Manchester)

RESISTANCE

The communists had dreams,
The communists, the communists.

Caetano Veloso

For Jorge Boccanera

The left doesn't arrive, the left isn't enough, can't see the end, the crossdresser. It sees nothing, neither the end of poverty nor its beginning. The right feeds on everything, everything is right in this world, a blind jaw that chews up its victims, falls calm, to swallow them down and collect for all eternity submission or a thoughtless vote. The little souls tricked by democracies' civics classes go seasoned and dressed to that set of onyx teeth. You won't be able to put up any walls or fences in a stomach as ferocious as that. When tyranny is a daily bleed that functions drop by drop and comes with sewer water in a certified container for nuclear waste, resistance is whispered, a pagan prayer, an exploding bomb travelling from a past war, the memory of Marx that cures all ravings but leaves us in Siberia or on a library shelf. Capital stored up in the blood is legal, mortal, eternal in the same hands as ever. *Capital* should be read like a Sutra. All labour is forced.

(Chetham's Library, Manchester)

EL ORDEN DE LO POCO

Salidos de la ruta principal, aparecen carteles escritos a mano con letra irregular, ofertas del día a la buena de dios o del que pase por este camino perdido de ciudades tan cercanas. Huevos de pato, pavo o gallina, verdura, productos de oficios pequeños que traen una pátina del mundo otro, tercero o cuarto. La mujer, con los pómulos quemados de sol y nieve, pregunta: "¿está muy pobre la gente en su país?" Envuelve la compra, orgullosa de su gallo, del cordero que muerde los bordes del cantero de rosas, de su pan que parece provenir de Tolstoi. Su voz aleja la palabra miseria pero renueva la palabra víctima. Pregunta qué pobreza tenemos nosotros, tan lejos, y sonríe sin dejarme responder, camino a su casa del fondo; mientras veo en su rostro la misma mirada de aquel mapuche que me ofreció un trozo de carne al otro lado del Atlántico. Sus ojos brillan igual, sin motivo aparente, ajenos a otro menester que no sea sobrevivir y proteger el orden de lo poco que hay.

(Armthorpe)

THE ORDER OF WHAT LITTLE THERE IS

Once off the main road, you see handmade signs in uneven writing, the day's offering by the grace of God or whoever's passing by, on a route lost to cities so close. Eggs – duck, turkey, or hen – veggies, products of small crafts that carry a hint of another world – the third or fourth. The woman, her cheekbones burnt by sun and snow, asks, "Are the people very poor in your country?" She wraps up the goods, proud of her cockerel, her lamb that nibbles the edge of the rose beds, of her bread that looks like something out of Tolstoy. Her voice pushes away the word destitute but revives the word victim. She asks what kind of poverty we have, so far away, and smiles without letting me answer, walking back towards her house; while I see in her face the same look of a Mapuche man who offered me a slice of meat on the other side of the Atlantic. Their eyes shine alike, with no apparent motive, alien to any task except surviving and protecting the order of what little there is.

(Armthorpe, South Yorkshire)

LA VIDA NATURAL

Algunos personajes de Berger – tal vez él mismo – parecen comprender la vida natural en medio de la civilización del lucro, y asumen la renunciación de quien vive igual que la vaca, que duerme con su amo durante el invierno para ser sacrificada con dolor y gozo en el verano. Recorro parcelas sucesivas donde no hay riqueza visible, pero la serenidad irradia desde un orden sin abundancias. El límite hacia abajo se traspasa en las parcelas divididas, en las casas clausuradas al frente para resistir en uno o dos cuartos, y ahí se huele desesperación tras las ventanas claveteadas. Una vivienda con su granero ha quedado como rehén entre las dos vías de la autopista, y los moradores hacen la labor, ajenos a las decenas de vehículos que pasan cada minuto. Dentro de cada máquina que cruza ese óvalo de tierra a velocidad contemporánea, los miembros de la familia duran un segundo como figuras de una película antigua, y desaparecen para siempre.

(M62, Leeds–Manchester)

NATURAL LIFE

A few of Berger's characters – perhaps even himself – seem to understand natural life in the midst of profit civilization, and resign themselves to living like a cow, sleeping with her master through the winter to be sacrificed with pain and pleasure come spring. I travel through plot after plot where there's no visible sign of wealth, but serenity radiates from an order without plenty. The boundary below crosses the divided plots, the houses closed up to hold fast in a couple of rooms, and there's a smell of desperation behind windows nailed shut. A house with its granary has been held hostage between the two lanes of the motorway, and the inhabitants do their work, alien to the dozens of vehicles that fly by each minute. Inside each machine that passes this oval of land at a modern-day speed, the members of the family last a second, like figures from an old movie, and disappear forever.

(M62, Leeds–Manchester)

EL CUIDADOR DEL OSO

Para Raúl Mansilla

El Circo del Estado de Moscú tiene función en Inglaterra. La comparsa dura más que el Estado de Stalin, su continuidad ignora el derrumbe de cualquier muro. Es de otro material o espíritu esta gente, no necesita lamentar gulags para divertir a Occidente. Es precario este Estado, un remedo que viaja lejos de su origen para mostrar lo que no tiene y sugestionar un poco a los presentes con prestidigitación y paraísos de cartón piedra al alcance del nuevo proletariado, que aquí aún paga la entrada. Quedan equilibristas, damas de a caballo y domadores de animales irreconocibles. Al circo le cuesta regresar a Moscú, y se sospecha que el viaje es un anuncio que se postergará para siempre. En los camarines del antiguo presentador, viejos banderines del Spartak; fotos de Gagarin y Trotsky. El público inglés aplaude a los animales por compasión, y el payaso ruso les resulta feroz. El cuidador del oso me dice que la vejez acosa al animal. Es lo único auténtico de este circo, insiste. Todo durará mientras viva ese animal de Siberia.

(Newcastle)

THE BEAR KEEPER

For Raúl Mansilla

The Moscow State Circus is performing in England. The troupe lasted longer than Stalin's State, its lifespan knows of the fall of no walls. These people are of a different matter or spirit, they don't need to apologise for the gulags to entertain the west. This State is precarious, a cheap imitation that travels far from home to show what it doesn't have and suggest something to those present with magic tricks and cardboard utopias within the reach of the new proletariat, who here still pay to get in. The acrobats, equestriennes, and animal tamers remain, unrecognisable. It's hard for this circus to go back to Moscow, and one suspects that it's a journey whose announcement will never come. In the dressing room of the former ringmaster, old Spartak pennants; snaps of Gagarin and Trotsky. The English audience cheers the animals out of compassion, and the Russian clown is too fierce for them. The bear keeper tells me that old age has beset the beast. It's the only thing authentic in this circus, he insists. It'll last as long as that Siberian creature survives.

(Newcastle-upon-Tyne)

LA LUCHA DE CLASES

What she read/All heady books/
She'd sit and prophesise/
(It took a tattooed boy from Birkenhead/
To really really open her eyes).

The Smiths

Las naves inmensas retumban ahora en el silencio. El espíritu de los alborotadores, los sufrientes, los que inspiraron a Marx, ha caído en el olvido junto a las maquinarias que los ataban. Todo lo sólido se desvanece en el aire, dijo, y advirtió sobre aquello que se sigue desvaneciendo en nosotros. Siglos amargos, revoluciones pervertidas, libros sagrados reducidos a ceniza. El siglo XXI liquida a los restos de la clase obrera con la incitación al suicidio. Las fábricas son refugios y no panópticos abandonados. Olvidados de luchar, ardientes contra el enemigo omnipotente e invisible, queda el desafío de recordar el grito y la ira. Cruzado el cuerpo por la desilusión, bebemos frente a la fábrica desahuciada, unidos por nada. Trabajadores despedidos de todo, perros que sueñan con carne, ociosos a la fuerza ante los diques repintados. Hasta caer, bebemos líquidos que saben a lo perdido, inmóviles en terrazas lustradas donde se simula la paz y la lucha de clases es el título del espectáculo de la verdad póstuma.

(Birkenhead)

CLASS STRUGGLE

What she read/All heady books/
She'd sit and prophesise/
(It took a tattooed boy from Birkenhead/
To really really open her eyes).

The Smiths

The immense boats echo now in silence. The spirit of the troublemakers, those who suffered, Marx's inspiration, has passed into oblivion like the machines they were tied to. All that is solid melts into air, he said, and warned us about everything that's still melting inside us. Bitter centuries, revolutions perverted, holy books reduced to ashes. The twenty-first century liquidates the remains of the working class by incitement to suicide. Factories are refuges and not abandoned panopticons. Forgetful of the struggle, burning against the all-powerful and invisible enemy, there's still the challenge of remembering the shouts and the rage. Bodies run through by disillusion, we drink in front of a moribund factory, united by nothing. Workers sacked from everything, dogs dreaming of meat, the forced idle faced with freshly painted dry-docks. Until we fall, downing drinks that taste of loss, immobile on shiny terraces where peace is feigned and Class Struggle is the title of a show about posthumous truth.

(Birkenhead)

EL ARTISTA PURO

El presente eterno, sin ídolos ni religión posible. Mamuts, cabras del monte, osos, leones, bisontes, panteras y búhos en la roca, venidos de la mano de artistas sin nombre, nacidos milenios antes de cualquier filosofía. La idea de futuro abolida junto con el lenguaje que podría construirla. Un espacio permanente de gracia, donde la lluvia de ayer no se convierta en el barro de hoy. La piedra es inocente y precisa; sin espejos donde mirarse ni idea de dios superior a una estrella o un relámpago. En este sitio queda la calavera del hombre superior a su memoria, el artista puro del tiempo de los animales. El origen perdido, no una caverna en sentido filosófico, sino la pulsión de hacer algo que entonces carecía de nombre y ahora llamamos 'arte'. La inocencia de representar lo cotidiano desconocido sin pretensiones ni interpretación, a galaxias de distancia de un museo del futuro.

(Altamira, lejos de la cueva auténtica)

THE PURE ARTIST

The eternal present, with no idols or religion possible. Mammoths, mountain goats, bears, lions, bison, panthers and owls on the rock, from the hand of artists without name, born millennia before any philosophy. The idea of the future abolished along with any language that could construct it. A permanent space of grace, where yesterday's rain won't become today's mud. The rock is innocent and precise; without mirrors to see yourself nor an idea of any god greater than a star or a lightning fork. Here lies the skull of a man greater than his memory, the pure artist from the time of animals. The lost order, not a cave in the philosophical sense, but in the impulse to do something that then had no name and today we call 'art'.[11] The innocence of depicting the everyday unknown with no pretence or interpretation, galaxies away from a future museum.

(Altamira, Spain, far from the real cave)

UNA FOTO EXTRAVIADA

La bahía de Rhossili es la más salvaje, desolada y
estéril que conozco, cuatro o cinco millas de frialdad
amarilla entrando en la distancia del mar.

Dylan Thomas

Para Diego Angelino

Al frente todo es cielo, horizonte desmesurado, lluvias que aún no alcanzan a vislumbrarse sobre la bahía perfecta. En la lejanía cabe, si no detenemos nunca la marcha, aquello que aún no hemos visto. Es un desvío, una bifurcación para perderse, el placer de aquel dolor intenso que pudimos conjurar, la recepción de un hotel antiguo, el polvo que levantaron nuestras huellas en el camino. Es Ella, no un recuerdo, otra cosa. Alejadas de uno, las marcas en la arena no desaparecen ni borradas por la marea. Es un hálito, una casa perdida en la montaña, una foto extraviada que ahora sí es recuerdo. Es eso lo que sostiene, al frente, el cielo. Nubes, aire gélido de otras tierras, nos queman los pulmones. No sabemos qué sostiene el horizonte en la vida inmóvil.

(Rhossili)

A LOST PHOTO

Rhossili Bay is the wildest, bleakest and
barrennest I know – four or five miles of yellow
coldness going away into the distance of the sea.

Dylan Thomas

For Diego Angelino

Ahead all is sky, enormous horizon, storms still out of eyeshot over the perfect bay. Fitting into the distance, if we don't halt our march, is everything we've not seen yet. A detour, a fork to get lost at, the pleasure of that pain we managed to conjure up, the reception in an ancient hotel, the dust our steps raised on the way. It's Her, not a memory, something else. At a distance, the marks in the sand don't disappear, not even when erased by the tide. It's a breath, a house lost in the mountains, a lost photo that now is a memory. Ahead of us, that's what holds up the sky. Clouds, frozen air from other lands, burn our lungs. We don't know what holds up the horizon in life at a standstill.

(Rhossili)

CONTRASEÑA

Quien ajusta miles de piezas al día, recoge goma en Sudán o cose en un taller clandestino. El que hace las joyas tecnológicas en turnos de 16 horas por un dólar. El niño que fabrica zapatillas aerodinámicas en Bangladesh, siempre descalzo. El que viaja en barca náufraga hacia los labios de Europa o huye de excéntricos criminales en África o Medio Oriente. Es un viaje en un territorio sin tiempo. No cruzan los mapas pensando en morir en manos de cualquier policía enmascarado, sino para bailar la danza grande de su origen en la oscuridad de un sitio secreto donde nadie podría apropiarse de su ritmo, que no pueden seguir sus represores. La frase no dicha, la palabra oscura irreductible, mágica o arcaica, eso llevan bajo sus andrajos como contraseña brillante de eternidad.

(Hamburgo)

PASSWORD

Someone who adjusts thousands of pieces a day, collects rubber in Sudan or sews in an underground sweatshop. Or who makes technological jewels working 16-hour shifts a dollar a time. The child making aerodynamic sneakers in Bangladesh, always barefoot. Or who voyages in a leaky boat towards the lips of Europe or flees eccentric criminals in Africa or the Middle East. It's a voyage in a land without time. They don't cross maps thinking they'll die at the hands of some masked policeman, but to move to the great dance of their homeland in the dark in some secret site where no one can steal its rhythm and their repressors can't go. The unspoken phrase, the dark and irreducible word, magical or archaic, is what they keep under their rags like a shining password to eternity.

(Hamburg)

LAS FORMAS DEL HAMBRE

Las planicies perfectas con su pasto universal sepultaron el aire de lecheros, ganaderos, mineros, contadores de historias al caer la noche y otros sobrevivientes que habitaban parcelas bajo este inmenso cielo perfecto. Refugiados malamente en los pueblos o reducidos a trabajadores rasos de los terratenientes nuevos, malviven de las sobras. La riqueza ajena tendió su manto de verde apisonado y envió al pasado quesos amarillos, pequeños rebaños de cara negra, viejos orgullosos que relataban lo que no debía perderse. El museo son sus cuencas oscuras, su mirada a un horizonte que ya no los abarca. Hay un dolor que atraviesa generaciones y corre por el caserío y la pradera como un ser mitológico de antes de las guerras de ahora, que matan por indignidad y por hambre real, pero también por hambre de otra realidad.

(Alston)

THE FORMS OF HUNGER

The perfectly-formed moors with their universal pasture entomb the air of dairy and cattle farmers, miners, dusk storytellers and the other survivors who occupy plots under this immense perfect sky. Taking scant refuge in the towns or reduced to base workers for the new lords of the land, they get by on scraps. Other people's wealth cast its cloak of trodden green and consigned to the past those golden cheeses, little flocks of blackfaces, proud old men who spoke of all that shouldn't be lost. The museum consists of their darkened hollows, their gaze at a horizon that no longer contains them. There's a pain that crosses generations and runs through the houses and the fields like a mythological being from before today's wars, that kill with indignity and real hunger, but also hunger for another reality.

(Alston, Cumbria)

PROFESORES TACITURNOS

El matadero global no repara en especies extrañas ni extremidades de colores diferentes, matices de la humanidad. Una cubeta de acero recoge sangre y esperma para vender en sacos esterilizados. La sangre de toda etnia es idéntica en apariencia, y el plasma cotiza en la bolsa. Se separan órganos internos de venta segura. Un hígado puede viajar de un cuerpo sano y miserable en Chechenia a otro enfermo y miserable en Nueva York. Algunos seres humanos se venden enteros. Rinden en talleres oscuros o camas donde son ultrajados sin distinguir sexo ni lengua. Sólo dicen ok en idioma universal y ofrecen carne al verdugo. Los niños califican. El carnicero global corta en segundos lo que sobra del tráfico y convierte lo demás en pasta alimenticia. Nada se tira, cada fragmento tiene su nicho de mercado. Los cadáveres que llegan tarde para la oferta de necrofilia son vendidos a las universidades. Algunos se diseccionan, otros se convierten en profesores taciturnos, con aires de provenir de una masacre.

(Colonia)

TACITURN PROFESSORS

The global slaughterhouse pays no heed to rare species or different coloured limbs, humankind's nuances. A stainless steel bowl collects blood and sperm for sale in sterilized bags. Blood of any race looks the same, and plasma has a price on the market. Internal organs can be separated out and easily sold. A kidney can travel from a healthy and wretched body in Chechnya to another one, sick and wretched in New York. Some human beings sell themselves whole. They work in sweatshops or beds where they're abused irrespective of sex or tongue. They say nothing except "OK" in a universal language and offer meat to the slaughterer. Children count too. In seconds, the global butcher slices traffic's leftovers and turns the rest into a nutritious paste. Nothing's wasted, each bit has a niche on the market. The corpses that arrive too late for necrophiliacs get sold to universities. Some are dissected, others turn into taciturn professors, with the air of having just got back from a massacre.

(Cologne)

MANUFACTURAS

Cocina árabe e hindú, turbantes y velos. Costureras, barberos, reparación de teléfonos, accesorios ilegítimos, frutas y verduras al borde de la calle, aromas mezclados de Oriente y la alcantarilla, gritos permanentes que remiten a Las mil y una noches. Un teatro Alhambra restaurado, malversada su estética original, y otro abandonado, bellísimo en su ruina. Factorías inmensas en las que dóciles inmigrantes envasan a ritmos de la revolución industrial lo que comerán confiados miles de europeos que desconfían de los extranjeros.

(Bradford)

MANUFACTURED GOODS

Arab or Indian food, turbans and veils. Dressmakers, barbers, telephone repairs, dodgy accessories, fruit and vegetables by the side of the road, mix of aromas from the East and the drain, constant shouting bringing memories of the 1001 Nights. A restored Alhambra Theatre, its original design betrayed, and another abandoned, beautiful in its ruins. Immense workshops where docile immigrants package, at the rhythm of the industrial revolution, food for thousands of trusting Europeans who distrust foreigners.

(Bradford)

UNA RELIGIÓN BOVINA

Pastan unas vacas marrones en parcelas que semejan jardines. Recostadas al atardecer sobre la hierba con su prosapia Shorthorn, miran con ojos profundos cual modelos de alta costura, aunque con su tonelada expuesta no se levantan para mostrarse. Estos animales de Yorkshire bostezan con signos de aburrimiento o melancolía, permanecen en su sitio sin alardes de animal. Nadie los arrea, todo el entorno conduce al sueño, la somnolencia, una religión bovina. Un viajero puede creer que las alimentan para completar el paisaje. Más que productos para la carnicería, completan piezas de un dispositivo de civilización que se afana con el decorado. En el cuadro de al lado, un grupo de ovejas de rostro negro parece posar para la secuencia que sigue, atentas de reojo a la pasividad de las vacas. Continúan con el rito de la mansedumbre, como si hubiera Paraíso. Sitios amables e inmaculados, en los que nadie imagina el matadero.

(Otley)

A BOVINE RELIGION

Some brown cows graze on plots that look like gardens. Resting on the grass as the day falls with their Shorthorn heritage and hollow eyes, they look like haute couture models, though with their tonnage on show they don't get up to parade. These Yorkshire animals yawn with signs of boredom or melancholy, they stay on their spot without animal showiness. No one drives them, the whole place leads to sleep, somnolence, a bovine religion. A traveller might think they're being fed just to complete the picture. Rather than products for butchering, they complete the pieces of a model of civilization keen on decoration. In the scene alongside, a group of black-face sheep seem to pose for the next sequence, eyes-wide open to the passivity of the cows. They continue the rite of the meek, as if there were a Paradise. Lovely, immaculate sites, where no one imagines the abattoir.

(Otley, West Yorkshire)

BELLEZA AJENA

Para Carolyn Riquelme, Bárbara Visnevetsky y Gerardo Burton

Pedazos, grandes trozos arrancados de tumbas, monumentos, templos de confesiones desconocidas, fragmentos que fueron parte de unidades concebidas para permanecer. Éste es un ritual antropófago e imperial, que olvida todo prurito de origen y arma de nuevo con planos viejos, reconstruye cada artefacto lejos del mundo particular en que ha nacido. Muestra como lujo superior la acumulación de belleza ajena, traída en barcos o traficada con el afán de la gloria o la placa de conmemoración. Todo ha sido rescatado para preservarlo de sus propietarios y las guerras banales en que han ocupado sus siglos, países inestables, culturas apenas advertidas de la belleza. Aquí se guarda, se pule, se conserva, con agradecimiento del mundo, el corazón disecado de cuatro continentes. Nadie llora por eso. Quienes nacieron en cada rincón donde moró un objeto en su origen llegan hasta aquí para mendigar un recuerdo, y se llevan una postal de su propio desamparo.

(Museo Británico, Londres)

OTHER PEOPLE'S BEAUTY

For Carolyn Riquelme, Bárbara Visnevetsky and Gerardo Burton

Pieces, great chunks torn from tombs, monuments, temples of unknown faiths, fragments that formed part of objects invented to last. This is a cannibal and imperial ritual, that forgets any discomfiting origin and constructs again with old plans, rebuilds each artefact far from the particular world in which it was born. It shows like a superior luxury the accumulation of other people's beauty, brought in boats or trafficked with the desire for fame or a commemorative plaque. It's all been salvaged to preserve it from its owners and the banal wars with which they've filled their centuries, unstable countries, cultures hardly conscious of beauty. Here, with the thanks of the world, they keep, polish and preserve the desiccated heart of four continents. No one cries for that. People born in those corners where these objects originally lived come here to beg for a memory, and take away a postcard of their own helplessness.

(British Museum, London)

LA POESÍA ELÉCTRICA

No quiero morir de esto: la mitad es convención
y la mitad es mentira.

Dylan Thomas

Para Lucía Boscá y Antonio Méndez Rubio

Sobre su silla, la poesía es eléctrica y está muerta. Su voz de cuello alcohólico y perfecto suena grisácea en este rincón de Gales donde él jamás encontró el lugar. Una máquina repite la grabación hasta abrumar de emoción, de pena por nosotros, que estamos memorando la muerte pasada o futura, siempre inevitable. La poesía se ha quedado sin destino, Dylan, por qué se piensa que un poeta tiene más futuro que un sepulturero o una chica que pasa. Tu voz es nuestra, surge de una tumba abierta con saña y anticipación, la poesía hecha para agradar a nadie con la intensidad de un fuego fatuo. No he querido ver el cementerio en que guardan tus restos menores, lo banal de tu vida en la tumba. El tamaño de la poesía de un país es equivalente al tamaño de su cementerio, decía Eliot. En este campo santo no cabe ninguna poesía, salvo la tuya.

(Laugharne)

ELECTRIC POETRY

By these I would not care to die
Half convention and half lie.

Dylan Thomas

For Lucía Boscá and Antonio Méndez Rubio

In his chair, poetry is electric and it is dead. His booze-throated, perfect voice sounds grey in this corner of Wales where he never found his place. A machine replays the recording until the emotion is spent, out of pity for us, who mark death, past or future, always inevitable. Poetry is left with no destiny, Dylan, why do people think that a poet has any more future than a gravedigger or a girl passing by. Your voice is ours, it rises from a tomb opened with cruelty and anticipation, poetry made to please no one with the flash of a will-o'-the-wisp. I didn't want to visit the cemetery where they keep your mortal remains, the banality of your life in the tomb. The size of the poetry of a country is the size of its cemetery, said Eliot. In this burial ground there's no room for any poetry, except yours.

(Laugharne, Carmarthenshire)

LENGUA DEL EXTRAÑAMIENTO

Para Fernanda Peñaloza y Chris Perriam

El viajero inglés se desplaza para terminar en un libro. Busca lo desconocido universal y se dedica a contarlo con palabras únicas para Inglaterra, el Mundo. Ese relato viaja por el planeta del idioma y el libro – que avizora lo útil con lo incógnito – lo acompaña. Todo será traducido para su lectura en Calcuta y Tierra del Fuego. Las descripciones habrán servido para que los habitantes del mundo descubran cómo deben contar su mundo a los viajeros. Aprendemos a fuerza de descubrir qué hay detrás del libro de un viajero inglés. Trabajamos sobre sus intersticios, relevamos pliegues de lo escrito, cavamos en Chatwin, vemos a trasluz la radiografía de Burton, somos arqueólogos de la palabra lejana. Un viajero sin lengua habla el extrañamiento, como los habitantes del extremo sur que Darwin hizo cruzar el Atlántico.

(Oxford)

LANGUAGE OF ESTRANGEMENT

For Fernanda Peñaloza and Chris Perriam

The Englishman travels to end up in a book. He seeks the universally unknown and sets to telling it with words unique to England, the World. That tale travels the planet of language and the book – spying the useful and the unknown – goes with it. It will all be translated to be read in Calcutta and Tierra del Fuego. The descriptions will help the inhabitants of the world discover how they should tell their world to travellers. We learn by force to uncover what is behind an English traveller's book. We work on its gaps, find folds in the writing, excavate Chatwin, hold Burton's X-ray up against the light: we are archaeologists of the foreign word.[12] A traveller with no language speaks estrangement, like those inhabitants of the far south who Darwin made cross the Atlantic.

(Oxford)

EL MODELO DEL CERDO

Un cerdo inmenso de ojos rojos mira el paso de los vehículos sobre un pasto de carpeta fina. El lote sobre el que reposa es minúsculo, se empequeñece en la escala del animal, que parece enmarcado para exposición entre muros ennegrecidos. La víctima carece de basura para masticar, y espera que le sirvan un sucedáneo, aditivos y cáscaras. El cerdo atisba la carretera con expresión de saber algo por encima de sus posibilidades. Comparte eso con el hombre que asoma, el desamparado que lo carneará. Los conductores pasan, sobrados de impaciencia, sin ver al inocente que los engordará hasta matarlos, ocupados en lidiar con animales de cultura que manejan el todo, la hora de regreso, el camino al cementerio, su rutina de bestias superiores sin dejar de ser esclavos, y también su dieta mortal.

(Richmond)

THE MODEL PIG

An immense, red-eyed pig watches the vehicles go past, on its green-baize grass. The plot it stands on is minute, made smaller by the scale of the animal, as if framed for exhibition between blackened walls. The victim lacks swill to chew, so it waits to be served a substitute, additives and peelings. The pig cautiously eyes the road with the expression of one who knows more than should be possible. It shares this with the man who appears, whose helpless job is to butcher it. The drivers go by, full of impatience, without seeing the innocent who will fatten and then kill them, busy battling with cultured beasts who run everything, clocking-off time, the way to the cemetery, their routine as higher animals, but still slaves, and their fatal diet.

(Richmond, North Yorkshire)

EL RASTRO DIGITAL

Productos de Pakistán, África subsahariana, corazón del Amazonas, sacudidos por el mar de la India y los aromas del mundo de los pobres, madera incógnita del sur de Chile, fugitivos de cada criminal que gobierna en los confines. Llegan empaquetados sin saber su destino, quedan en los cuerpos las marcas del embalaje. Corredores de fondo del Cono Sur, blindados de dureza, engañados por traficantes ilegales y de los otros, no son del todo pasto para las fieras. Llegan escorados, con la cara contra el barro, dispuestos al silencio, casi sin respiración. Trazan un rastro digital por los mapas, vigilados desde lo alto. Los sacude el Atlántico o el Mediterráneo y los recibe un ejército. Traen, debajo del manto de miseria, el brillo que reluce bajo los harapos. Un seleccionado de presos del sistema golpea platos y cucharas contra las ventanas de chapa buscando que algún familiar reconozca sus voces. Su hambre ha nacido después de todos los saqueos.

(Aluche)

THE DIGITAL TRACE

Products from Pakistan, sub-Saharan Africa, the heart of Amazonas, shaken by the Indian Ocean and the aromas of the world of the poor, unknown wood from the south of Chile, fugitives from all those criminals who rule on the margins. They arrive packaged without knowing their destination, marks of the wrapping still on their bodies. Long-distance runners from the Southern Cone, plated with strength, tricked by illegal and other traffickers, aren't just thrown to the lions. They arrive listing, faces against the mud, tending to silence, almost not breathing. They mark a digital trace on maps, tracked from above. Shaken by the Atlantic or the Mediterranean, an army waits for them. Under their blanket of poverty they shine just as bright under rags. A selection of the system's prisoners rattles plates and spoons against the metal bars looking for a relative who might recognise their voices. Their hunger was born after the pillage.

(Aluche, Madrid)

EL ROSTRO

Lamentablemente, el futuro ya no es lo que era.
Leyland Kirby

Anacrónico y elegante, el rostro de Guevara preside el barrio donde los derrotados izan la bandera última de una libertad ilusoria y por eso permanente. Todo ha envejecido aquí, pesados siglos transcurridos en décadas, aunque algo fluye, un furor a medias que excede todo aquello que pueda llamarse religión, furia, esas cuestiones. Aquí el rostro más regurgitado del siglo XX ha encontrado un lugar fuera de los artilugios del mercado.

(Derry)

THE FACE

Sadly, the future is no longer what it was.

Leyland Kirby

Anachronistic and elegant, the face of Guevara presides over a neighbourhood where the defeated raise the last flag of a freedom so illusory it's permanent. Everything has aged here, heavy centuries gone by in decades, although something flows, a half-way fury that surpasses anything that could be called religion, rage, those sort of questions. Here the most regurgitated face of the twentieth century has found a place untouched by the gimmicks of the market.

(Derry)

EL DOLOR QUE ACUNA

No busques comienzo ni fin de una historia de dolor. Hay algo detrás que será siempre empobrecido por una explicación. De un extremo a otro de la calle católica, cuando el sonido de la muerte acumulada late demasiado velozmente, cruzo al barrio protestante. Aquí los mártires son otros, las pinturas de otros héroes se multiplican, cambian las banderas, la miseria es la misma. Quién podría desprenderse de todo el dolor que acuna, sin sentir que el mundo desaparecerá por eso, para siempre, con la belleza adherida. Los sitios de asistencia al suicida se yerguen en calles protestantes y católicas. La muerte acecha, ahora por defecto, no por exceso.

(Calles Shankill y Falls, Belfast)

THE PAIN THEY CRADLE

Don't look for a beginning or an end to this story of pain. There's something behind that's always cheapened when explained. From one end to the other of the Catholic street, when the sound of death piled up beats too quickly, I cross to the Protestant side. Here there are different martyrs, the paintings of other heroes multiply, the flags change, the poverty stays the same. Who could let go of all the pain they cradle, without feeling that the world will disappear with it, forever, with all the beauty too. Suicide prevention centres spring up on Protestant and Catholic streets. Death lurks, by default now, not from excess.

(Shankill and Falls Roads, Belfast)

EL MECANISMO DE LA RIQUEZA

He estado soñando con un tiempo en que los ingleses estén
hartos
de los laboristas y los conservadores, y escupan sobre el nombre
de Oliver Cromwell, y denuncien a esta línea real que aún le
alaba, y le alabará por siempre.

Morrissey

Máquinas, máquinas, objetos que revelan el ingenio y la destreza infinita de la civilización del lucro. Brillan cuidadas con esmero como creaciones supremas, deidades de la era de las herramientas. Una taxonomía impecable las hace resplandecer; son creaciones sucesivas del siglo que perfeccionó la explotación humana. El museo muestra y oculta, destaca y envía al pudridero de la memoria aquello que no quiere ser mostrado a las conciencias fugaces. Estos objetos funcionaban hasta dieciocho horas al día a partir de las manos de obreros, algunos de brazos delgados como cuchillos, mujeres y hombres; nadie había quedado bajo el sol durante la creación mítica del capitalismo. Sus rostros muertos y sus brazos quebradizos han sido eliminados prolijamente. Podrían ocupar modestos retratos bajo el rostro de los propietarios, orgullosos al costado de sus máquinas con atributos de éxito mundial. Hasta un fragmento de espacio se les ha negado. No ha quedado ni imagen lejana de aquellos anónimos que hacían funcionar como una música el mecanismo de la riqueza ajena.

(Museo de Ciencia e Industria, Manchester)

THE MECHANISM OF WEALTH

I've been dreaming of a time when the English are sick to death
of Labour, and Tories and spit upon the name
Oliver Cromwell and denounce this royal line that still salute
him,
and will salute him forever.

Morrissey

Machines, machines, objects that reveal the ingenuity and the infinite skill of profit civilization. They shine, painstakingly cared for like supreme beings, deities from the tool age. An impeccable classification makes them gleam; they are creations in sequence from the century that perfected human exploitation. The museum shows and hides, picks out and consigns to the rubbish heap of memory anything that doesn't want to be shown to fleeting consciences. These objects worked up to eighteen hours a day with the hands of workers, some with arms thin as knives, women and men; there was no one left under the sun during the mythical creation of capitalism. Their dead faces and breakable arms have been carefully rubbed out. They might occupy a modest portrait under the face of the owners, proud alongside their machines with their global success. The merest shard of space is denied them. There's not even a distant shot of the nameless who made music on the mechanism of someone else's wealth.

(Museum of Science and Industry, Manchester)

NOMBRES IMPROPIOS

Halleluja!
It works.
We blew the shit out of them.

Harold Pinter

Cuál es la guerra justa. Ninguna música deja de sonar patriótica en la parodia, ni las banderas retienen categoría de símbolo, pero todos disparan desde su escondrijo o vuelo no tripulado. Cómo los hombres de espíritu pierden la independencia en medio de los gritos de cuervo de la diplomacia. Escribir es la cuestión, Adorno El Viejo, viendo Kabul, Sabra, El Tinduf o Katyn. Todos, nombres impropios. Pronunciados en la distancia no ocurre nada, aunque en el centro del horror su peste suena. El costo estándar del minuto de guerra no importa. La tortura no. La electricidad en la planta de los pies, espinas bajo las uñas, la bolsa en la cabeza, la picana creada en Francia para Argelia, en USA para Vietnam, en URSS para Polonia. Perfeccionada en el Cono Sur a fuerza de desaparecidos. Universal en Asia y África para llegar a Abu Ghraib. Qué deja de ser una guerra ahora, declarada o no, si cada avión sin matrícula ni bandera porta a sus torturadores en el limbo del cielo prometido a los culpables.

(Dieppe)

IMPROPER NAMES

Halleluja!
It works.
We blew the shit out of them.

Harold Pinter

Which is the just war. All music sounds patriotic in parody, as flags lose their status as symbol, but they all fire from their hideout or unmanned flight. How men of spirit lose their independence in the midst of the crow-calls of diplomacy. To write is the question, Old Adorno, faced with Kabul, Sabra, Tindouf or Katyn.[13] They are all improper names. Pronounced at a distance nothing happens, though in the centre of the horror their plague can be heard. The average cost of a minute of war doesn't matter. Torture doesn't. Electricity on the soles of the feet, splinters under nails, a bag over the head, the cattle prod created in France for Algeria, in the USA for Vietnam, in the USSR for Poland. Perfected in the Southern Cone on the disappeared. Ubiquitous in Asia and Africa before arriving at Abu Ghraib. What act isn't war today, declared or otherwise, if every unmarked, un-flagged plane in the limbo of the promised sky takes the guilty to their torturers.

(Dieppe)

LA VIDA SIN MASTICAR

Aquí en las arcadas quemadas de los centros comerciales, en las
comisarías selladas, en las ciudadelas perdidas del consumismo
puede encontrarse la verdad, nuevos territorios pueden abrirse,
puede haber una ruptura en esta amnesia colectiva.

Laura Oldfield Ford

El que no entiende que sabe, quien dice sí a otros y entrega su vida
sin masticar. El que come las palabras sin haber sido educado para
ellas, y deja su corazón en boca náufraga. El que escribe con un
lenguaje extraño a sí mismo, y olvida que detrás suyo resuenan
voces de otros que ruegan que los escriba. Una lengua u otra, le
dicen ellos, no hace diferencia; siempre que esa lengua nos escriba
a quienes no tenemos palabra alguna.

(Estación de Peckham Rye)

UN-CHEWED LIFE

Here in the burnt out shopping arcades, the boarded up precincts, the lost citadels of consumerism one might find the truth, new territories might be opened, there might be a rupturing of this collective amnesia.

Laura Oldfield Ford

Someone who doesn't understand that he knows, who says yes to others and hands over his un-chewed life. Someone who eats his words without having been taught to use them, and leaves his heart in a shipwrecked mouth. Someone who writes in a language that's strange to itself, and forgets that behind him other people's voices speak, begging him to write them down. One language or another, they tell him, what's the difference; as long as that language writes those of us who have no word at all.

(Peckham Rye Station)

UNA SOLA LÍNEA

Para Alba y Diego Angelino

El libro verdadero desaparece, se convierte en folleto religioso o bono de circo que regalan en la estación de trenes. Ese papel, tinta, objeto, apenas se asemeja al símbolo agonizante que antes se usaba como camino incierto pero probable de luz. En mi país enterrábamos libros igual que a cadáveres; su capacidad de fuego solía llevarnos a la muerte. Los asesinos quemaban libros junto a sus dueños, en nombre de la civilización de Occidente y de Cristo. El alma se quema. El libro desaparece. Textos vuelan de incógnito con fulgor de relámpago. Si queda una conexión entre nosotros y nuestras palabras, algo brilla. Otras evoluciones del ser son las que importan. El libro será escrito por todos, no por uno, como Lautréamont decía en la ciudad sitiada de Montevideo. Ahora lo siguen en África y otros agujeros nuestros, encadenando una palabra como línea para escapar de las cárceles. El libro desaparece y una sola línea perdura entre todos los dedos que la escriben.

(Hay-on-Wye)

JUST ONE LINE

For Alba and Diego Angelino

The true book disappears, it turns into a religious pamphlet or a circus discount given away in railway stations. That paper, ink, object, looks barely like the dying symbol that once was used as an uncertain path to probable light. In my country we used to bury books like corpses; their flammability could be a cause of death.[14] The murderers burnt books alongside their owners, in the name of the civilization of the west and of Christ. The soul burns. The book disappears. Texts fly into the unknown with a flash of lightning. Other evolutions in being are what matters. Books will be written by all, not by one, as Lautréamont said in the besieged city of Montevideo. Now they follow him in Africa and other holes we've made, chaining a word like a line to escape from jails. The book disappears and just one line lasts among all the fingers that write it.

(Hay-on-Wye)

LA TAREA DIARIA

El joven asistente recorre las salas dando cuerda a los relojes. Esa es su tarea diaria en este monumento al tiempo inútil o recobrado, el pasado y el presente en un silencio que pesa varios siglos. Lo hace con verdadero cuidado, se mueve levemente entre libros encuadernados en cuero antiguo, esquiva pequeñas mesas y pisa alfombras con la misma delicadeza con que alguno de los habitantes originales debió caminar por aquí, con recato y un vestuario de pedrería y prejuicios.

(Harewood)

THE DAILY CHORE

The young employee goes from room to room winding up the clocks. That's his daily chore in this monument to useless or regained time, past and present in a silence that weighs several centuries. He does it with genuine care, moving slowly among the books bound in ancient leather, avoiding little tables or stepping on rugs with the same delicacy with which one of the original inhabitants would have trod around here, with caution and outfits full of precious stones and prejudice.

(Harewood House, West Yorkshire)

SIN MALICIA

Los pueblos convertidos al turismo ejercen su doble vida. En un tiempo propio suspenden este siglo en otro anterior, o en dos. En el espacio dedicado a seres dispuestos a ver el campo en rápidas sesiones, fruncen el ceño para servir una muestra de su saber estar en silencio. Sus ancestros les legaron la sabiduría de permanecer impasibles ante la tormenta o el paso de las estaciones, y mover el cuerpo con gracia suficiente para que el trabajo duro aparente una danza. Ilustran sobre la huerta, animales y elixires con rictus de antiguos cultivadores de tiempo. Se resisten a ser mayordomos, y eligen la observación de las nubes y el pronóstico de sequías y lluvias reparadoras. Esperan el regreso del atardecer y aguardan ruidos que reaparecen con el silencio. Cuando los visitantes parten, hablan de ellos sin malicia, como quien describe a un animal extraño, de hábitos incomprensibles pero fatales. La velocidad del instante no cabe en la suspensión de su memoria.

(Amberley)

WITHOUT MALICE

Towns turned to tourist sites live their double life. In a time all of its own, they suspend this century in another from before, or in two. In the space devoted to those beings prepared to see fields in rapid sessions, they furrow their brows to offer a show of their skill at falling silent. Their ancestors left them the knowledge of how to stay impassive faced with storms or passing seasons, and to move with enough grace to make hard labour look like a dance. They illustrate the farm, animals and elixirs with the rictus of ancient farmers of time. They refuse to be butlers, and choose to observe the clouds or forecast droughts or reparative rains. They await the return of the afternoon and the noises that reappear with the silence. When the visitors leave, they talk about them without malice, like someone describing a strange animal, with incomprehensible but fatal habits. The speed of the instant can't fit in the suspension of memory.

(Amberley, West Sussex)

LOS CALAMBRES

Spanish songs in Andalucía
The shooting sites in the days of '39
Oh, please, leave the ventana open
Federico Lorca is dead and gone.

Joe Strummer (The Clash)

El muro ha caído con el paso del tiempo y los inviernos crudos, pero ya había sido esqueleto agujereado por los disparos. Los verdugos lo preferían por su altura, para que las familias vieran morir en directo a los condenados desde las exiguas ventanas de su mente. A pocos metros, un pequeño monte guarda un círculo de vegetación ausente, y un tronco cortado perdura como mesa a juzgar por los cortes profundos y antiguos. El árbol se ve como se verían los cuerpos talados en vida. Allí comerían su botín robado, su pan con aceite, los fusiladores. Así descansarían entre tiro y tiro, y calmarían en la fuente los calambres del dedo percutor.

(Pozos de Víznar)

CRAMPS

Spanish songs in Andalucía
The shooting sites in the days of '39
Oh, please, leave the ventana open
Federico Lorca is dead and gone.

Joe Strummer (The Clash)

The wall has fallen with the passing of time and the raw winters, but it was already a skeleton holed by the shots. The executioners preferred it for its height, so that the families would see the condemned die, live from the little windows of their minds. A few metres away, a low hill still has a circle stripped of vegetation, and a cut-down tree trunk survives like a table, to judge by the deep and ancient cuts. The tree looks like the bodies must have looked, chopped down in life. There the shooters would eat their stolen booty, their bread with oil. A way to relax, between shots, and to soothe in the fountain their trigger-finger cramps.

(Barranco de Víznar Mass Graves, Granada, Spain)

UN CAMINO INFINITO

Para Zara Hasnaui, Bahía Awah, Salem Bachir
y el pueblo saharaui

La mente del que viaja por tierra calcinada es siempre una carga. El que sabe dónde hallar el agua subterránea, la senda escondida en la arena, los túmulos de piedra dejados con intención para quienes saben verlos. El que vive pendiente de la sombra esquiva, el que sabe la ciencia de ocultarse sin correr hacia el espejismo. El desprotegido que arde por dentro hasta sangrar: esa sangre se convierte en su conocimiento. Su duda es el margen de la libertad: si se equivoca muere, si no distingue la ensoñación del oasis muere también. El desierto es un país donde la muerte aguarda en silencio. Una mirada intensa devuelve un horizonte sin marcas, un camino infinito carente de guía.

(Plaza de Yamaa El Fna, Marrakesh)

AN INFINITE PATH

To Zara Hasnaui, Bahía Awah, Salem Bachir
and the Saharaui people

Travelling across scorched earth, a mind is always a burden. Someone who knows where to find water underground, the hidden track in the sand, the tumuli of stones left on purpose for those who know how to see them. Someone whose life depends on the shifting shade, who knows the science of hiding without running towards the mirage. Unprotected, the burning inside turns to bleeding: that blood turns into his knowledge. His doubt is the margin of freedom: a mistake means death, and if he can't tell the daydream from the oasis he dies too. The desert is a country where death waits in silence. An intense gaze returns the unmarked horizon, an infinite path with no guide.

(Place Jemaa El Fna, Marrakesh)

LA FOTO DE LAS VÍCTIMAS

La guerra en los museos imperiales es dolorosa para el cerebro vencido. Las víctimas toman imágenes de una guerra, la suya, lloran con ellas en el regazo o buscan a sus familiares en la pila de víctimas de las fotos oficiales. La guerra se multiplica en los museos, ordenados para acumular muestras de la victoria y restos de las víctimas. Patos embalsamados, fieras de todos los continentes, soldados ajenos como bichos pequeños, muertos, con la cabeza gacha de derrota. Las maquetas, con millares de combatientes del tamaño de una aceituna, fuerzan un dolor inversamente proporcional. Una secuencia infinita de paciencia delicada, miles de objetos creados para producir daño y muerte, la delicadeza del entomólogo, la restauración impecable, el movimiento como al acecho de los cuidadores, el ambiente preparado para que cada arma tenga su contexto, su guerra particular, su víctima propiciatoria.

(Imperial War Museum)

THE PHOTO OF THE VICTIMS

War in empire's museums is painful for the defeated brain. The victims carry images of a war, theirs, crying with them on their lap or looking for their relatives in the pile of victims in the official photos. War is multiplied in museums, arranged to pile up evidence of victory and the remains of victims. Embalmed ducks, beasts from all continents, foreign soldiers like little animals, dead, with bowed heads of defeat. The scale models, with thousands of combatants the size of olives, force an inversely proportional pain. An infinite sequence of sophisticated patience, thousands of objects created to produce damage or death, the care of an entomologist, an impeccable restoration, as if the movement were watched over by the curators, the atmosphere prepared so that each weapon has its context, its particular war, just the right victim.

(Imperial War Museum, London)

UN BALÓN FALSIFICADO

Algunos vecinos pensaron, sin duda, que era chocante
que la vida sea valuada menos aún que una mercancía.

Lord Byron

La clase obrera ya no obra fuera de la obediencia. Sin acción ni máquinas para romper, el metal y el sindicato escasean, hay plástico de computadores y gabinetes de atención telefónica. Ni ludditas ni marxistas, ven el fútbol en suburbios de casas iguales, eludiendo la hipoteca o el desalojo. Gritan goles contra todos, a favor de un equipo que representa a millonarios. Los niños de la clase obrera sueñan con coartadas que los lleven a la mafia o la fortuna. No hay campos suficientes para lanzar balones contra el capitalismo, sino rectángulos de césped donde se ejercitan los hijos de otros colegios. No alcanzan las bicicletas para recorrer el mundo como niños italianos de la posguerra o perseguir animales como si pastaran en América o el África subsahariana. Si pudieran, lanzarían contra la llamada sociedad o economía mundial ese balón falsificado que aprietan contra el pecho y por momentos parece una bomba a punto de activarse.

(Tottenham)

A COUNTERFEIT BALL

Some folks for certain have thought it was shocking,
That Life should be valued at less than a stocking.

Lord Byron

The working class no longer works except in obedience. Without action or machines to break, metal and the union are scarce, there's the plastic of computers and telephone helplines. Neither Luddites nor Marxists, they watch football in suburbs with their identical houses, evading mortgages or eviction. They cheer goals against everyone, for a team that represents millionaires. Working class children dream of alibis to join the mafia or money. There aren't enough pitches to shoot balls at capitalism, only grass rectangles where children from other schools exercise. Bicycles aren't enough to travel the world like post-war Italian kids or to chase animals like shepherds in the Americas or sub-Saharan Africa. If they could, they'd kick against so-called society or the global economy, kick that counterfeit ball that they clutch to their chests and at times looks like a bomb about to explode.

(Tottenham)

COME DE TODO

Clama un discurso dominante: Marx ha muerto, el comunismo está muerto, bien muerto, con sus esperanzas, su discurso, sus teorías y sus prácticas, ¡viva el capitalismo, viva el mercado, sobreviva el liberalismo económico y político!

Jacques Derrida

La fortuna es propia de los otros, los que deben el mundo al mundo pero no aceptan cuentas pendientes de pago. El capital sólo llega en cantidades suficientes a manos adecuadas que saben destruir, multiplicarse, volver a destruir diques o límites que le pongan. Come de todo el capitalismo sin fin, vomita y vuelve a comer, todo es carne fresca para el apetito suyo, los animales de los siglos fueron hechos para su hambre de comer en movimiento animales vivos, familias enteras. El capital hace su propio trabajo al devorar y reunir cantidades infinitas, pero nunca hará el tuyo ni dejará de beber de tu sudor. El capital no es egoísta, pero no puede desprenderse de sí mismo.

(Edimburgo)

FEEDS ON ANYTHING

This dominant discourse proclaims: Marx is dead, communism is dead, very dead, and along with it its hopes, its discourses, its theories, and its practices. It says: long live capitalism, long live the market, here's to the survival of economic and political liberalism!

Jacques Derrida (trans. Peggy Kamuf)

Fortunes belong to other people, who owe the world to the world but won't accept late payments. Capital only arrives in sufficient quantities in the right hands, who know how to destroy, multiply, destroy once more, the dykes or barriers put in its way. Endless capitalism feeds on anything, vomits and feeds again, it's all fresh meat for its appetite, the animals of the centuries were made for its hunger to eat on the move, live animals, whole families. Capital does its own work as it devours and brings together infinite quantities, but it will never do yours or stop drinking your sweat. Capital isn't selfish, but it can't let go of itself.

(Edinburgh)

LA DANZA EFÍMERA

Para Osvaldo Costiglia

El pato se zambulle de espaldas a la obra más perfecta de Henry Moore. Sale del agua y vuelve a sumergirse, y no mira jamás hacia el acero que refleja belleza sin decrepitud. El pato está en su danza efímera, casi perfecta. No sabe que será tierra también, quizás acero esculpido, o si quedará en un tiempo como simple materia descompuesta. Ajenas al pato y a Moore, ovejas elegidas para pastar entre esculturas mordisquean un pasto que sabe común, y mezclan su estiércol con la eternidad.

(Yorkshire)

THE FLEETING DANCE

For Osvaldo Costiglia

The duck dives with its back to Henry Moore's most perfect work. It emerges from the water and then dives again, and doesn't look back towards the steel that reflects beauty with no decrepitude. The duck is there in its fleeting, almost perfect dance. It doesn't know that it too will be earth, perhaps sculpted steel, or if with time it'll just end up as simple decomposed matter. Indifferent to the duck and to Moore, sheep chosen to graze among sculptures nibble a pasture that tastes common, and mix their dung with eternity.

(Yorkshire)

SUENA UNA MÚSICA LEJANA

Para Andrés Cursaro y Ariel Williams

Se viaja para huir del día utilitario, de la vida útil y reglada, pero también del viaje convertido en parte de un recorrido previsible. Suena una música lejana y aquí estamos, sin guía ni legado, ni las prescripciones del que visita lugares para encontrar aquello que ya ha sido clasificado. Viajamos para no regresar iguales, y perder en el viaje nuestra razón y los hábitos calcados en la mente. Regresamos, llenos o vacíos, a reparar los agujeros de nuestras palabras, que hemos gastado tanto.

(Montaione)

HEAR A DISTANT MUSIC

For Andrés Cursaro and Ariel Williams

Travel is a way to flee the utilitarian day, the useful, regulated life, but also from travel itself turned into a predictable path. You can hear a distant music and here we are, with no guide or legacy, nor the prescriptions of someone who visits places to find the already classified. We travel to come back different, to lose on the journey our reason and the ingrained habits of the mind. We return, full or empty, to mend the holes in our words, which we've worn out so much.

(Montaione, Tuscany)

REZAR A UN SUPERHÉROE

Pedirle a un dios es llorar ante mármol desnudo. Los ritos superpuestos dejaron su recuerdo entre las paredes de los templos y las marcas de los disparos sobre los muros. El guion repetido de los guías. El aire ya no se lleva los hedores. Tu amor, tu dolor, el verbo dislocado de quienes creían rezar a un superhéroe que no escuchaba los lamentos. La mente de quienes describen una masacre repetida como canción de cuna. ¿Importan las masacres que se repiten, la descripción del dolor infinito? Sueño algo peor que una promesa incumplida: sueño lo que existe.

(Lourdes)

PRAY TO A SUPERHERO

To ask something of a god is to cry before naked marble. The clashing rites left their memory inside the walls of temples and the marks of gunshot on the walls. The guides and their reread script. The air that no longer removes the stench. Your love, your pain, the dislocated word of those who thought they prayed to a superhero who didn't hear their cries. The mind of people who describe a repeated massacre like a lullaby. Do they matter – the massacres that repeat over, the description of infinite pain? I'm dreaming of something worse than an un-kept promise: I'm dreaming of what exists.

(Lourdes)

LA BENDICIÓN DEL BÚHO

La imagen del búho, un pájaro específico que suena lejano en el tiempo pero está susurrando al otro lado de la calle, en el amanecer de los árboles del vecino. El animal entrevisto al cerrar sus alas como un monje, imaginado en los años del símbolo, vuela sobre un lago de sangre vertida por mí mismo, en dosis desiguales, a lo largo de un viaje por toda la vida. No descenderá el pájaro en este charco pasajero, pasará sobre él sin purificarlo. No beberá de él. Mi vida depende del vuelo de ese pájaro, solo me sirve aguardar despierto su bendición fugaz antes de perderse en el horizonte.

(Calle Cumberland, Leeds)

THE OWL'S BLESSING

The image of the owl, one bird in particular that sounds far away in time but is whispering on the other side of the street, in the dawn of the neighbour's trees. The animal half-seen as it closes its wings like a monk, imagined over the years as a symbol, flies over a lake of blood shed by itself, in unequal doses, the length of a journey through a whole life. The bird won't land in this passing pool, it will fly over without purifying it. It won't drink from it. My life depends on the flight of this bird, all that's left for me is to wait wide awake for its fleeting blessing before it disappears over the horizon.

(Cumberland Road, Leeds)

MERECER EL CAMINO

El paseo oscuro, todo aquello que no sabemos ver, puro atisbo. La caída, cada vez, en lo que ya éramos, no en lo que íbamos a buscar. Aprender del camino es dejar el saber para escuchar la sabiduría que no tiene certeza de aceptación. En cada sitio, invisible para quienes pasan presurosos hacia nada, mora un sujeto que aprendió demasiado. Aprendió a callar su dolor o herida para convertirla en otra forma de silencio. Esa gracia se busca en cada desvío o recodo, en cada parada presuntamente innecesaria. En la posada de luces amarillas al final de la senda, en el desvío del mercado, persiste un objeto o idea que nunca tendrá precio o intérprete. Cuando te acerques podrás intuir su existencia para justificar tu paso por el camino que lleva a ninguna parte. Caminar, caminar, para merecer el camino.

(Malham)

EARN THE PATH

The walk in the dark, everything that we can't see, the barely glimpsed. The fall, every time, into what we already were, not into what we were looking for. Learning from the path means abandoning knowledge to listen to the wisdom that has no guarantee of acceptance. In every spot, invisible to those who hurry past towards nothing, lives a subject who learnt too much. Who learnt to keep quiet about their pain or wound to turn it into another form of silence. That gift is sought in each detour or bend, in each presumably unnecessary stop. In the yellow-lit inn at the end of the track, in the detour in the market, an object or idea survives that will never have a price or an interpreter. When you get closer you'll be able to sense its existence in order to justify your steps along the path that leads nowhere. Go on, go on, to earn the path.

(Malham, North Yorkshire)

TRANSLATOR'S NOTES

1. Hesperidina: an Argentine orange-flavoured liqueur.
2. *Mate* is a popular type of tea in the Southern Cone region; typically it is drunk from a dried, hollowed out gourd through a metal straw.
3. Ernesto Che Guevara's nickname comes from the Argentine habit of addressing people as 'Che', roughly equivalent to 'hey' or 'man' in English.
4. References to Bruce Chatwin and to Osvaldo Bayer – both chroniclers of Patagonia, one internationally famous, the other with a more limited reputation, but of great importance to Aliaga's vision of the South.
5. There is a pun in the Spanish that is difficult to capture: *salvar* is 'to save' but it also has a less common meaning of 'to cover or cross [a distance]'.
6. *Motivo* is both an artistic motif and a motive, or reason.
7. Julio Argentino Roca (1843-1914), Argentine general and later president, leader of the so-called 'Campaign of the Desert' of Argentine southern expansion against first-nation peoples.
8. The city of Antofagasta in northern Chile developed largely because of its importance in saltpetre/nitrate mining. Previously part of Bolivia, it was captured during the War of the Pacific (between Chile, Bolivia and Peru) and officially handed to Chile in 1904.
9. *Conciencia* is both awareness and conscience in Spanish.
10. *Legado* is both a legacy or inheritance and a [papal] legate.
11. A reference to Plato's image, as voiced by Socrates in *Republic*, of a pre-historic cave wall, on which shadows are cast, as an analogy for human beings' untutored perception of the world.
12. Burton: the explorer and writer Richard Francis Burton.
13. References to the Sabra and Shatila massacre, West Beirut, 1982; the Tindouf refugee camps for Western Saharan exiles in Algeria; and the Katyn massacre of Polish prisoners over several months in 1940.
14. This is a reference to the 1976–1983 dictatorship in Argentina, when people burnt or buried 'suspicious' books – from Marxist theory to Jewish cookery recipes – out of fear that these might be seen as – potentially fatal – evidence in case of a police or military raid.

INDEX OF PLACE NAMES

Printed and bound by CPI Group (UK) Ltd, Croydon, CR0 4YY

13/02/2023

03191168-0002